UTSA DT LIBRARY RENEWALS 458-

A Practical Guide to
PROGRAM EVALUATION PLANNING

WITHDRAWN
UTSA LIBRARIES

D1040444

WITHDRAWN
UTSA LIBRARIES

A Practical Guide to
PROGRAM EVALUATION
PLANNING
Theory and Case Examples

Editors
Debra J. Holden
RTI International
Marc A. Zimmerman
University of Michigan

Los Angeles • London • New Delhi • Singapore • Washington DC

Library
University of Texas
at San Antonio

Copyright © 2009 by SAGE Publications, Inc.

All rights reserved. No part of this book may be reproduced or utilized in any form or by any means, electronic or mechanical, including photocopying, recording, or by any information storage and retrieval system, without permission in writing from the publisher.

For information:

SAGE Publications, Inc.
2455 Teller Road
Thousand Oaks,
California 91320
E-mail: order@sagepub.com

SAGE Publications India Pvt. Ltd.
B 1/I 1 Mohan Cooperative
Industrial Area
Mathura Road, New Delhi 110 044
India

SAGE Publications Ltd.
1 Oliver's Yard
55 City Road
London EC1Y 1SP
United Kingdom

SAGE Publications
Asia-Pacific Pte. Ltd.
33 Pekin Street #02-01
Far East Square
Singapore 048763

Printed in the United States of America

Library of Congress Cataloging-in-Publication Data

A practical guide to program evaluation planning: theory and case examples/editors, Debra J. Holden, Marc A. Zimmerman. — New ed.
    p. cm.
Includes bibliographical references and index.
ISBN 978-1-4129-6775-4 (pbk.)
    1. Evaluation research (Social action programs) 2. Social service—Evaluation. 3. Educational evaluation. I. Holden, Debra J. II. Zimmerman, Marc A.

HV11.P673 2009
361.2072—dc   222008020275

This book is printed on acid-free paper.

08 09 10 11 12   10 9 8 7 6 5 4 3 2 1

Acquisitions Editor:	Vicki Knight
Editorial Assistant:	Lauren Habib
Production Editor:	Carla Freeman
Copy Editor:	Trey Thoelcke
Typesetter:	C&M Digitals (P) Ltd.
Proofreader:	Susan Schon
Indexer:	Michael Ferreira
Cover Designer:	Arup Giri
Marketing Manager:	Stephanie Adams

Library
University of Texas
at San Antonio

CONTENTS

PREFACE

After conducting so many diverse evaluations, we came to realize that our training, though excellent on many levels, had not really prepared us for what happens behind the scenes. We learned about research designs in applied settings, controlling for the many potential confounding factors in evaluation research, process evaluations, issues of fidelity, and many other design issues. Yet we did not really expect that so much of an evaluation design is determined by the work that happens before the evaluation design is even discussed. As our community partners have noted, we learned that evaluation research required an intervention before the intervention. This realization inspired us to consider a conceptual framework to guide this pre-evaluation work that is required for a successful evaluation. This work has been termed *evaluation planning,* and researchers are beginning to pay more attention to this issue. Our Evaluation Planning Incorporating Context (EPIC) model extends this previous work to include some of the political and contextual issues that are inevitably a part of every evaluation. We also noticed in our own evaluation work that settings may differ in terms of the specific planning issues to consider but that all had some pre-evaluation issues with some common themes that required attention before we could even begin to think about the evaluation design, measures, and procedures for carrying it out. We invited several colleagues with experience conducting evaluation in different settings to discuss the background work they had to do for their case examples. We asked them to discuss that work using our EPIC model to provide a consistent analysis of similar issues across settings. We hope that the EPIC model will be a useful guide to those conducting evaluations and that the case examples will help bring the EPIC model to life across evaluations that involve schools, service programs, community organizations, and media.

ACKNOWLEDGMENTS

The editors wish to acknowledge their families. Debra Holden would like to acknowledge Richard and Jacob Cowart for their love and tolerance of her long working hours. Marc Zimmerman would like to acknowledge Debby, Ben, and Sarah, whose support and patience make all he does possible. Both would like to acknowledge the expert editorial work of Susan Murchie at RTI International.

We would also like to thank the following reviewers for their helpful and constructive suggestions. Their input led to a much improved book.

Rhonda Cockerill
University of Toronto

Lena M. Lundgren
Boston University

Cynthia A. Tananis
University of Pittsburgh

1

INTRODUCTION

Debra J. Holden and Marc A. Zimmerman

A Practical Guide to Program Evaluation Planning provides a framework to guide evaluators as they begin developing a program evaluation. As Rossi, Lipsey, and Freeman (2004) note, program evaluation involves the "use of social research methods to systematically investigate the effectiveness of social intervention programs in ways that are adapted to their political and organizational environments and are designed to inform social action to improve social conditions" (p. 16). Though several authors have written books on how to conduct an evaluation, few have addressed the issues that an evaluator faces before implementing the evaluation (e.g., establishing the design and measures or collecting the data). In this book, we use the term *evaluation planning* to refer to the process that occurs prior to implementation. In this context, planning involves stating the purpose of the evaluation, understanding the organizational and political context in which the program operates, determining the evaluation uses, working with stakeholders to identify the primary and secondary evaluation questions, and ensuring stakeholders' buy-in of the evaluation regardless of its ultimate results.

Building on the first three steps of the Centers for Disease Control and Prevention (CDC) "Framework for Program Evaluation in Public Health" (1999), we have developed a conceptual model called Evaluation Planning Incorporating Context (EPIC). The EPIC model provides a plan for addressing issues in the preimplementation phase of program evaluation. Though books on evaluation research cover design and measurement issues, few authors have addressed the extent to which an evaluator needs to understand the program context when approaching an evaluation. For example, Rossi et al. (2004) and Patton (1997) briefly discuss some of the important issues to consider during evaluation planning, but they do not provide guidance on the steps an evaluator may need to consider in determining the evaluation design and measures.

In planning effective program evaluations, we have realized that attention to issues prior to implementation and assessment of the context within which the program operates is critical to the evaluation's success. *Context* is defined as "the set of circumstances or facts that surround a particular event, situation, etc." (Dictionary.com, n.d.). With respect to program evaluation, context includes all of the underlying factors surrounding the program, including the level of support among organizational leaders and staff (and sometimes consumers) for the evaluation and the expected uses of the evaluation results by program management. These factors may vary from one context to the next and may be influenced by a range of issues related to the organizational and political environment within which the program evaluation is to occur. These issues also affect the people who should be selected to participate in the evaluation planning process (i.e., stakeholders) and the questions the evaluation will address.

We begin the book by presenting our five-step EPIC model: (1) assess context, (2) gather reconnaissance, (3) engage stakeholders, (4) describe the program, and (5) focus the evaluation. We present these as steps because this progression is efficient and informative for subsequent phases of planning and implementation, but they are not necessarily completed in linear fashion. Our own experience suggests that these phases can occur in a different order, overlap, or be reconsidered and adapted throughout the planning process.

In the first step, assessing context, we note the importance of the evaluator gaining a thorough understanding of the unique environment and people involved in the program and how they may influence critical information about the program. Key issues to address during this step include defining the relationship between the evaluator and the sponsor and determining the level of the evaluation. For the evaluator and sponsor relationship, determining the degree of independence of the evaluator's role is important. In many cases, the evaluator is to conduct an "independent evaluation" of the program so that the findings will be completely unbiased. This type of independent evaluation is typically led by an evaluator external to the sponsoring organization. However, the extent to which the evaluator is to operate independent of the sponsor in planning and implementing the evaluation needs to be understood up front. In situations where the evaluation is to be conducted by an evaluator internal to the organization, an important issue to address is ensuring that the evaluator remains objective during the planning process and does not impose his or her own agenda into the final plan.

The level of an evaluation affects the types of variables that will need to be incorporated into the evaluation plan. *Level* refers to the focus of the evaluation in terms of whether the findings of greatest interest are at the individual level (i.e., the people served by the program), community or local level, state or regional level, or national level. Each level of evaluation will have different contexts that the evaluator needs to understand thoroughly to effectively plan the evaluation. The differing levels, for example, will influence the selection of stakeholders to engage in the evaluation planning process and the questions that will be of greatest importance to the sponsor.

The second step of the EPIC model, gathering reconnaissance, involves understanding and getting to know all of the people engaged in the evaluation plan. These people may include leadership of the sponsor organization, key stakeholders (e.g., program staff, community leaders, or clients of the program), and partners involved in program implementation. As the evaluator works to understand the relationships among all of the involved people, he or she needs to specify all the ways in which the evaluation findings are expected to be used. For example, the evaluation results may be used to revise the program operation, obtain additional funding to expand the program, or terminate the program. After involving interested parties to determine the evaluation's uses, the evaluator should validate perspectives with the sponsor to resolve conflicting expectations, assess management commitment to the evaluation, and confirm understanding of evaluation parameters.

During the evaluation planning process, the evaluator identifies potential stakeholders to engage in the evaluation (the third step of the EPIC model). Often, the sponsor has a list of people to include as stakeholders, and the evaluator may identify others to include in the planning process. Depending on the uses of the evaluation findings, these stakeholders may need to include policymakers who ultimately will decide whether the program continues after the results are available. Once the stakeholders have been identified, the evaluator needs to work with the sponsor to define the stakeholders' roles in the planning process and establish a process for obtaining systematic and timely input.

The fourth step of the EPIC model, describing the program, involves learning about all facets of the program and identifying the underlying concepts behind the program's goals and objectives. During this step, the evaluator may develop tools to help convey his or her understanding of the program. For example, a conceptual framework or logic model provides a visual depiction of program components and how they are hypothesized to work together to achieve short- and long-term outcomes. Another tool, the evaluation planning matrix, specifies the evaluation questions and the corresponding outcomes and data sources. The purpose of the matrix is to identify data needs and sources, identify gaps in available data, and provide guidance in the prioritization of evaluation questions during the final step of the EPIC model.

In the final step of the EPIC model, focus the evaluation, the evaluator leads a process to finalize the evaluation plan. At this point, the evaluator should have a comprehensive list of potential evaluation questions and outcomes to include in the final evaluation plan. Once this list is complete, a process begins to prioritize the evaluation questions that can actually be answered within the time and resource constraints for the evaluation. This process most often includes the stakeholders. Another factor to consider when prioritizing evaluation questions is the feasibility of the data collection and whether it would impose an undue burden on program staff, take too long to conduct, or answer the questions of greatest importance to the sponsor and stakeholders.

We propose that each of these five steps is important in planning for a program evaluation within any context, but the time allotted for evaluation planning will greatly affect the degree to which the evaluator can complete all phases of an evaluation adequately. The context also will determine whether the issues described in Chapter 2 are even relevant to a particular evaluation planning process.

To present the diversity of possible program evaluations, we invited authors who conducted evaluations in different contexts to describe their evaluation planning experiences. We asked them to frame their descriptive analyses in terms of the EPIC model presented in Chapter 2. The evaluators describe case examples of evaluations conducted in a school setting (Chapter 3), a service agency setting (Chapter 4), a community-based program (Chapter 5), and for a national media campaign (Chapter 6).

In Chapter 3, "Planning for an Education Evaluation," Dr. Julie Marshall applies the EPIC model to the planning process for an evaluation of the Integrated Nutrition Education Program in Denver, Colorado. The organizational and political context within a school system is particularly complex and unique. Stakeholders in this setting can range from school board members, district or school administrators, and teachers to parents and their children. Understanding the relationships between the key stakeholders and establishing a process for engaging them is important for an evaluator in an educational setting to ensure that stakeholders perceive that they have a voice in the ultimate outcomes. Through the evaluation planning process, the evaluator ultimately will be best prepared to focus the evaluation and streamline the specific outcomes so that all stakeholders are confident their input has been incorporated into the final evaluation plan when feasible.

In Chapter 4, "Planning for a Service Program Evaluation," Dr. Mari Millery applies the EPIC model to the planning process for an evaluation of a local chapter of the Leukemia & Lymphoma Society (LLS). The context within a service setting is influenced by the types of services provided, the clientele, and the agency's intended uses for the evaluation findings. In assessing the context within a service setting, the evaluator needs to learn a great deal about the agency within which the program is operating and the political climate relevant to the evaluation. For a service agency, the uses of the evaluation, as determined through Step 2 (gathering reconnaissance), can sometimes inform the decision whether to continue or terminate a program. Though this can be the case for an evaluation within any context, programs within a service agency can be directly tied to the jobs of people engaged in the planning process, and the evaluator needs to be sensitive to these issues. It is therefore especially important for the evaluator to ensure that the data collected are valid and as rigorous as possible given time and funding constraints. In this setting, the evaluator must be particularly sensitive to ensuring the feasibility of the proposed data collection, because staff members within the agency are often expected to collect the data. In the case of LLS, data were collected from clients as they called in for services; therefore, Dr. Millery needed to ensure that staff could be trained to collect the prioritized measures within the time they had contact with clients.

In Chapter 5, "Call and Response: Developing a Collaborative Evaluation Plan for a New Community-Based Program," Dr. Thomas Reischl and Susan Franzen present an evaluation planning process for a community-based program, the African American Family Resource Information Center and Network (AFRICAN). Because AFRICAN was developed through collaborations with a large number of community-based organizations, the processes of assessing the context for the program, especially with regard to the evaluator's relationship with the sponsor, and engaging stakeholders were particularly important. The lead author, Dr. Reischl, played a dual role as a voting member on committees and as an evaluator; thus, potential conflicts of interest needed to be addressed with the sponsor prior to the evaluation. In addition, the authors note that with this type of evaluation in particular the evaluator needs to be very client-centered and cognizant of the stakeholders' perspectives with regard to the evaluation. A process was followed to engage each partner in evaluation planning and ensure that outcomes of interest for most of them were incorporated into the final plan.

In Chapter 6, "Planning for a Media Evaluation," Dr. W. Douglas Evans, Dr. Matthew Farrelly, and Kevin Davis describe the planning process for an evaluation of a national antismoking media campaign called truth®. Planning for a media evaluation is unique for an evaluator, with so many potential audiences and messages that may be considered for the campaign. For the truth® campaign, the evaluators note the need to thoroughly understand aspects of health communications messaging and delivery to evaluate the impact of potential advertisements adequately. In this case, assessing context involved understanding the extent to which the target audience was exposed to the campaign and how the degree of exposure was related to campaign outcomes. Gathering reconnaissance involved thoroughly understanding the intent of the campaign's sponsors in the messages they wanted to deliver and how they thought their campaign was going to directly result in specified outcomes. This type of knowledge was particularly important when focusing the evaluation on deciding which key constructs to incorporate into the final plan.

The case studies in this book provide examples of the range of issues associated with applying the EPIC model in a variety of contexts. We acknowledge that there is significant variation even within a specific evaluation context, and that evaluation may occur in many other settings that are not addressed here (e.g., business settings, government agencies, and global organizations). Nevertheless, we chose the settings represented in the chapters to help readers develop a better understanding of the various steps that need to be taken in planning for an evaluation before the evaluation design is completed. The quality and usefulness of these evaluations were directly related to the effort and attention paid to the many background issues depicted in our EPIC model. Evaluation must be tailored to the specific program being evaluated, and the context of that program plays a significant role in the evaluation that is eventually implemented. This book provides the guidance needed to better organize and plan for program evaluations in common settings within which many evaluators work.

REFERENCES

Centers for Disease Control and Prevention. (1999). Framework for program evaluation in public health. *Morbidity and Mortality Weekly Report, 48*(RR11), 1–40.
Dictionary.com. (n.d.). *Context.* Lexco Publishing Group. Retrieved February 27, 2008, from http://dictionary.reference.com/browse/context
Patton, M. (1997). *Utilization focused evaluation: The new century text.* Thousand Oaks, CA: Sage.
Rossi, P. H., Lipsey, M. W., & Freeman, H. E. (2004). *Evaluation: A systematic approach* (7th ed.). Thousand Oaks, CA: Sage.

2

EVALUATION PLANNING HERE AND NOW

Debra J. Holden and Marc A. Zimmerman

The process of developing a comprehensive evaluation plan that meets the four evaluation standards of integrity, feasibility, usability, and propriety (Joint Committee on Standards for Educational Evaluation, 1994) can be quite complex and tedious. In many ways, this process is an art form that relies heavily on the evaluator's intuition, perceptions, and ability to assess what will best address the concerns of those involved in the evaluation (i.e., sponsors and stakeholders) and provide the outcomes of greatest use and interest. As Rossi, Lipsey, and Freeman (2004) note, the evaluation should be guided by a thorough analysis of the context within which it will occur. This book focuses on the process for assessing that context and incorporating it into planning using a variety of evaluation approaches. This book focuses on the issues that evaluators need to consider before and during the planning process as they determine the approach and design they will use in conducting an evaluation. This chapter provides a framework for thinking about the evaluation planning process that is used in subsequent chapters, which apply these ideas to specific case examples.

BACKGROUND ON EVALUATION PLANNING

In 1999, the Centers for Disease Control and Prevention (CDC) published the "Framework for Program Evaluation in Public Health," which was developed by numerous evaluators with experience evaluating programs in public health, education, and other areas. Figure 2.1 shows the six steps in CDC's framework for program evaluation, including three steps that could be considered specific to evaluation planning (although the authors provide

7

little detail about the process to follow for that planning): (1) engage stake-holders, (2) describe the program, and (3) focus the evaluation plan. Within this framework, we present the issues for evaluators to address during the evaluation planning process. In addition to the first three steps of the frame-work presented in Figure 2.1, we describe two additional preplanning steps that we have termed *assess context* and *gather reconnaissance*. Together, these five steps make up our Evaluation Planning Incorporating Context (EPIC) model (see Figure 2.2).

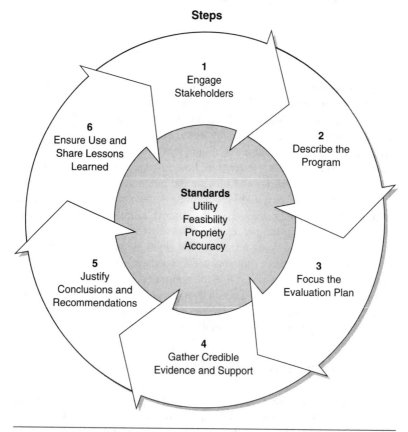

Figure 2.1   CDC Framework for Program Evaluation

SOURCE: CDC (1999).

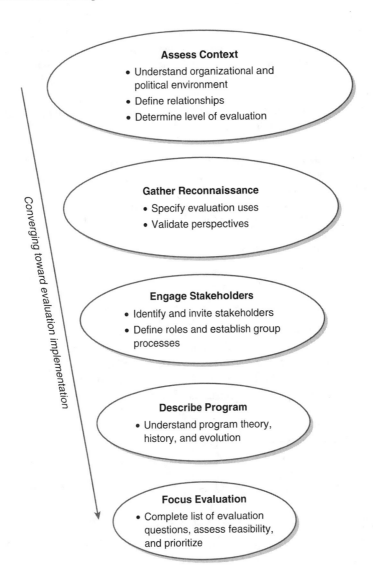

Figure 2.2　Evaluation Planning Incorporating Context (EPIC) Model

During each step in the planning process, the evaluator must consider a number of issues to determine which evaluation design best fits the context and is most suitable and feasible (see Table 2.1). As shown in Figure 2.2, this process leads the evaluator to the point of focusing the evaluation such that he or she is prepared to begin implementation. In addition to the issues summarized in Table 2.1, the evaluator must consider the available resources. As noted by Rossi et al. (2004),

> The evaluation plan must accommodate the inevitable limitations on the resources available for the evaluation effort. The critical resources include not only funding but also the time allowed for completion of the work, pertinent technical expertise, program and stakeholder cooperation, and access to important records and program material. A balance must be found between what is most desirable from an evaluation standpoint and what is feasible in terms of available resources. (p. 61)

ASSESS CONTEXT

A successful evaluation is not only useful, practical, ethical, and accurate, but it is also informed by an understanding of the special characteristics and conditions of each particular program. The evaluator needs to plan and conduct the study in the context of the program's people, politics, history, resources, constraints, values, needs, and interests (Patton, 1997). Table 2.1 shows three distinct issues to address in assessing the context: (1) understanding the organizational and political environment, (2) defining the relationship between the evaluator and the sponsor, and (3) determining the level of the evaluation. These issues are described in detail in the following subsections.

Understand the Organizational and Political Environment

The American Evaluation Association (AEA) *Guiding Principles for Evaluators* (2006) states that a key principle for the conduct of an evaluation is to obtain a comprehensive understanding of the sociopolitical context of the evaluation. Researchers have noted that it is critical to understand the political context of an evaluation (Weiss, 1973), while also attending to organizational issues such as the structure and circumstances of the program being evaluated (Rossi et al., 2004). To build on this previous work, we propose three specific features of the organizational and political

Table 2.1   Issues to Address During Each Step in the Planning Process

Steps in the Planning Process	*Description of Planning Step*	*Issues to Consider During Each Step*
Assess Context	Evaluator thoroughly understands the environment within which the program and evaluation occur.	• Understand the organizational and political environment. • Define the relationship between the evaluator and the sponsor. • Determine the level of the evaluation.
Gather Reconnaissance	Evaluator informally learns about relationships among stakeholders and partners.	• Specify the uses of the evaluation findings. • Validate perspectives related to the evaluation.
Engage Stakeholders	Evaluator invites key stakeholders and establishes structures and lines of communication to facilitate their involvement.	• Identify and invite stakeholders. • Define stakeholder roles and structure for their input. • Establish group processes for ongoing stakeholder input.
Describe the Program	Evaluator thoroughly describes and conceptualizes the program.	• Conceptualize program theory or rationale. • Understand program history and evolution.
Focus the Evaluation	Evaluator establishes domains of greatest interest to finalize focus of evaluation.	• Complete comprehensive list of evaluation questions. • Ensure feasibility (including burden of data collection) of answering questions. • Prioritize questions to include in the final evaluation plan.

context that evaluators should learn about prior to contacting stakeholders and gaining an in-depth understanding of the program:

1. Organizational infrastructure within which the program operates
2. Stage of program development
3. Political environment within which the evaluation will be conducted

Organizational Infrastructure

Understanding the organizational infrastructure supporting a program to be evaluated is essential to knowing how high of a priority that program is to the organization's ongoing efforts. It is vital to understand such issues as where the program resides within the organizational structure, how many staff members have time allocated to work on the program, and what level of management is involved in the program's operation and oversight. These factors can all indicate how important the evaluation is to the organization and can help the evaluator explore potential evaluation uses. An evaluation may be required by governmental funding guidelines, but the program being evaluated may be so small and inconsequential to the overall mission and vision of the organization that the findings are of little consequence. Understanding these types of factors before the planning effort can help the evaluator develop an evaluation that is useful, relevant, and maintains scientific integrity.

Stage of Program Development

Evaluations can differ dramatically depending on the stage of program development at which the evaluation is to be conducted. An evaluation conducted prior to program implementation is more likely to be formative in nature by informing stakeholders of aspects of the program that are working well or could be improved. In contrast, an outcome evaluation, or an evaluation that "gauges the extent to which a program produces intended improvements in the social conditions it addresses" (Rossi et al., 2004, p. 58), will involve a different approach to evaluation design and measurement. Cronbach (1991) specified several stages of program development, from the "breadboard" stage when the program has been "provisionally incorporated into field activities on a small scale" to the "operating program" stage when the "program is permanently up and running" (p. 336). The evaluation context is also considerably different if the findings will be used to justify continued funding of a program; this scenario can also impose significant time constraints on the evaluator if planning and conduct of the evaluation have to occur within a short time (Bamberger, Rugh, & Mabry, 2006). A thorough understanding of where the program is in its development and the purpose of the evaluation is essential for addressing many of the other issues in the planning process.

Political Environment

Evaluators should also consider the political environment within which the evaluation will be conducted to help identify the explicit and implicit motivations and purposes of the evaluation. If the program is at the end of its funding cycle and the evaluation is to provide justification for continued funding, then understanding the political investment in the program is critical to ensuring that appropriate measures are captured in the evaluation. For example, tobacco control is an issue that many states have been attempting to address politically with widely varying degrees of success. In North Carolina, a leading tobacco-producing state, tobacco control is an emotionally charged issue because reductions in smoking can directly affect local farmers and the communities in which they live. An evaluator working on a tobacco control program in North Carolina needs to be aware of the political and societal issues surrounding tobacco production and use in order to incorporate an understanding of the effects of the program on the community and to attend to unintended consequences of implementing the program. One example would be an evaluation of a statewide tobacco control initiative implemented in counties where a high volume of tobacco farmers reside. To be able to provide findings on how the statewide efforts are affecting tobacco farmers and their economic well-being, such an evaluation would ideally incorporate outcomes related to the economic effects of tobacco control on local farming establishments. These outcomes may not be specific program objectives but would be critical to include in the evaluation in order to attend to the sociopolitical context in which the program operates. Other politically charged issues, such as adolescent pregnancy prevention, reproductive health, and HIV prevention, may also be especially affected by the context within which the evaluation is conducted. Therefore, it is critical to understand relevant political issues and take them into account in program evaluation planning.

Define the Relationship Between the Evaluator and the Sponsor

The evaluation purpose is directly related to the evaluator's relationship with the sponsor. As noted by Rossi et al. (2004), an "often neglected but critical aspect of an evaluation plan involves spelling out the appropriate relationship between the evaluator and the evaluation sponsor and other major stakeholders" (p. 62). Rossi et al. describe three types of evaluator–sponsor relationships:

1. Independent evaluation, in which the "evaluator takes primary responsibility for designing and conducting the evaluation."
2. Participatory or collaborative evaluation, in which the "evaluation is conducted as a team project involving stakeholders."
3. Empowerment evaluation, in which the "evaluation is designed to help develop the capabilities of the participating stakeholders in ways that enhance their skills or political influence" (p. 62).

In addition to these possible relationships, the evaluator's role in the planning phase includes being a negotiator. Patton (1997) points out that negotiating the role an evaluator plays is an important step to take with the primary users of the evaluation. In the context of role definition, the issue of independence is an aspect of the evaluator's role that requires attention early in the evaluation planning process. How independently the evaluator is to operate and provide findings is directly related to the assumed validity of the ultimate findings. This issue is a particular challenge when the evaluator is working internally for the evaluation sponsor. Because of the potential of undue pressure on an internal evaluator, many sponsors require that an evaluation be conducted by an "independent evaluator" to ensure that the evaluator has no stake in the evaluation results. With this independence comes assumed objectivity, which can enhance how the findings are interpreted. If an evaluator is independent of the program, then stakeholders may be more likely to accept the findings as objective and valid. Therefore, this independence can enhance the credibility of both the evaluator and the ultimate evaluation results.

However, some sponsors have difficulty encouraging the evaluator's independence because they have such a large stake in the results and may fear that independence will result in negative findings for the program. Thus, the experience of the evaluator is critical. Evaluators with applied experience in the topic under study and in the system within which it operates can lend knowledge and credibility to the evaluation that is otherwise difficult to capture (e.g., an evaluator who formerly worked in a state health department on the staff of a cardiovascular health program and is now evaluating a similar program in another state). An evaluator with relevant experience who can operate independently is ideal, but this cannot always be accomplished due to timing, staffing, or budgetary issues. Evaluators with a stake in a program, and who therefore are not independent, may need to take special steps to establish the objectivity of their evaluation, such as serving on the advisory board to oversee all aspects of the evaluation; providing regular updates on evaluation activities to stakeholders; and identifying an external expert (or expert panel) to verify the design, procedures, and data. It is vital to define the relationship between the evaluator and the interactions expected with the sponsor prior to initiating the evaluation planning process. However that relationship is defined (e.g., independent, collaborative), the negotiating skills of the evaluator will come into play in determining ways to enhance independence and minimize interference.

Determine the Level of the Evaluation

"Level" of evaluation is a fairly complex concept that refers to the perspective of greatest importance to be measured through the evaluation. For example, a program that is being evaluated at the local level will involve different stakeholders and measures than a program that is being evaluated at the national level. The level of an evaluation is often difficult to understand or communicate to the sponsor and requires some education for the sponsor. One way to think about level is in terms of aviation: Is the evaluation to be conducted from a view 30,000 feet above sea level or from on the ground?

This concept is best explained with an example. A number of evaluations conducted for CDC have involved defining the level of evaluation early in the planning process. CDC is a government agency that provides funding to state, tribal, territorial, and other agencies and organizations to implement public health programs addressing a variety of public health concerns. When CDC provides program funding, it is commonly distributed to state health departments, which in turn provide funding to state partners or local health departments and organizations, which then implement the program. When conducting an evaluation sponsored by CDC, one of the first questions to address as an evaluator is which level of outcome is of primary interest. In other words, if the evaluation is to focus on work 30,000 feet above sea level, then the focus will be on assessing CDC's effectiveness in administering the program, assessing CDC's interactions with partners and awardees, or determining the outcomes CDC hopes to achieve with the program under study. However, CDC may be more interested in program-level outcomes, with a view 15,000 feet above sea level, and wants to characterize and understand how the states are implementing the programs. The purpose of the evaluation and outcomes of interest to the sponsor drive the level or focus of the evaluation. If the outcomes of interest are more behaviorally based, such as increases in a desired health behavior, the level of the evaluation would be more local (i.e., "on the ground") and would need to focus on developing questions and measures at the individual level. Often, the evaluator needs to incorporate more than one level (e.g., both state and local) into the evaluation plan. It is important for the evaluator to know in which situations the level needs to be defined and use that information to engage stakeholders and create appropriate evaluation questions and methods.

GATHER RECONNAISSANCE

Specify Evaluation Uses

Evaluations are almost always funded for specific purposes. In the eight-step process first described by Wholey (1978), an evaluator needs to determine the uses of any subsequent evaluation information in order to effectively plan for and design an evaluation. Patton (1997) identified three uses of evaluation findings: "rendering summative judgments; improving programs formatively; and generating knowledge about generic patterns of effectiveness" (p. 118).

Though evaluators are not the ones to determine whether a program is worthwhile or what actions to take based on the results, they should be aware of how policymakers could use their findings. It is also quite possible that the sponsors have not considered how to use the findings, and in such cases the evaluator needs to educate stakeholders on the possible uses of the results. It may also be necessary to work with stakeholders to identify both intended and unintended results produced by the program. Though the evaluator cannot control how the information will be used, planning for the application of evaluation findings can help guide the design, define resources needed to carry out the design, and shape the final report. In addition, this information can help establish relationships, define expectations, and set the tone for the evaluation.

Validate Perspectives

As Patton (1997) has described, a "common error made by novice evaluators is believing that because someone has requested an evaluation or some group has been assembled to design an evaluation, the commitment to reality testing and use is already there. Quite contrary, these commitments must be engendered (or revitalized if once they were present) and then reinforced throughout the evaluation process" (p. 37). Some evaluations are legislated as part of a program, supported by the program's external advisory board, or driven by the funding agency and do not have the complete support of the program administrators. Thus, prior to initiating the planning process, the evaluator needs to determine whether the sponsor's management staff support the evaluation and how they expect to use the findings. Evaluation reports are sometimes ignored because the people who were initially committed to the evaluation leave the program before the evaluation is completed, management staff decide the findings are not important to use in implementing policy change, or the overall organization loses interest in what the evaluation could tell them about the program. As Patton (1997) notes, "Evaluation is an unnatural act . . . that's why they need professional assistance, support, training, and facilitation" (pp. 37–38). It is the evaluator's role to provide that support and ensure that stakeholders, and in particular program management staff, understand the utility of the evaluation and the potential uses of its findings. In some cases, the evaluator may also help develop strategies to utilize evaluation findings, or the evaluator may be called on to clarify how the evaluation can be useful, explain the purposes of the evaluation, or help reconcile competing expectations of the evaluation results.

ENGAGE STAKEHOLDERS

Stakeholders are important team members in the development of an evaluation plan because they are generally experts in the program itself and understand how it can affect the funding source or local community. The stakeholders of a specific program evaluation vary, and identifying who they are greatly depends on the steps taken to assess the context and gather reconnaissance. As described in Chapters 3 through 6 of this book, who the stakeholders are and the extent to which they are involved also varies depending on the evaluation approach. For example, a community-based evaluation of a new school-based program may invite stakeholders who are lay members of the community to be a part of the evaluation planning process. Some suggest that it is best to involve stakeholders before or at the same time that the evaluator becomes involved and to continuously engage them throughout the evaluation (Reineke, 1991).

Identify and Invite Stakeholders

Identifying who the key stakeholders are for a specific evaluation is a critical process. Some have referred to this process as identifying the evaluation's consumers or audience (Rossi et al., 2004). Key stakeholders are defined as individuals who are affected by or involved in the program under study (Patton, 1997). Possible stakeholders include the following:

- Evaluation sponsors
- Decision makers or program champions
- Program management and staff
- Program clients
- Community members

Because most evaluations include multiple stakeholders in various levels of program development and/or implementation who will be affected by the evaluation results, the evaluator needs to carefully assess which stakeholders to involve and what role they will play. Stakeholders can be organized in different ways and involved in several roles. The evaluator may need to be creative in identifying which stakeholders to involve, specifying their role, and defining the time frame for their involvement. Depending on the evaluation, key program staff may be more involved in the evaluation planning and early phases of evaluation (e.g., process or formative), whereas stakeholders external to the program have a stake in findings later in the evaluation (e.g., political leaders, users of the program). It is important to include representatives of all the relevant evaluation audiences in the planning process. In scenarios where the program or issue under study is politically charged, engaging stakeholders outside of the program early in the planning stages is critical for achieving useful evaluation findings. As Cronbach (1982) notes, "in a politically lively situation . . . a program becomes the province of a policy-shaping community, not of a lone decision maker or tight-knit group" (p. 6). In these situations, it may be important to interview stakeholders such as community leaders or elected officials to obtain their input as to what is important to know about a particular program so that corresponding measures can be included in the evaluation. Table 2.2 provides examples of the types of stakeholders who can be involved and the nature of their involvement in planning and conducting the evaluation.

It is important to keep in mind as these roles and expectations are developed that the process of engaging stakeholders may require a great deal of time and resources. Two strategies to ensure that time is well spent are proactively defining the roles and expectations of the stakeholders prior to engaging them in evaluation planning and establishing a process for ongoing engagement as the evaluation is implemented.

Define Stakeholder Roles and Structure for Their Input

In determining who to invite as a stakeholder, the evaluator needs to define the role of the stakeholders in terms of the degree to which their input will be incorporated into the evaluation plan and their ongoing involvement in the evaluation once it is implemented. Clearly specifying expectations for involvement, both initially and throughout the evaluation, helps develop trust between the evaluator and the stakeholders. Much of the literature on evaluation focuses on the involvement of stakeholders early

Table 2.2   Examples of Possible Stakeholder Roles and Nature of Involvement

Type of Stakeholder Involved	Role in Evaluation Planning	Nature of Involvement
Academicians/ content experts, evaluation experts	Advise on evaluation design, measures, methods, and interpretation of results.	Once evaluation questions are specified, provide advice on proposed data collection, methods, and measures; ultimately assist in interpreting findings.
Staff working directly with the program, either in management or in local implementation	Inform each step of evaluation planning.	Provide perspective on purposes and uses of the evaluation, assist in program description and identification of stakeholders, and provide input into creating and prioritizing evaluation questions.
Potential program clients/participants	Advise on focus of the evaluation.	Provide participant's perspective on the important aspects of the program to be assessed to inform focusing of the evaluation questions.
Community members and local leaders	Ensure incorporation of context into evaluation plan, advise on focus of the evaluation, and help plan application of results.	Provide input from the larger community on how the program under study fits in with other work being done; advise on focus of the evaluation.

in the planning process to ensure that the evaluation meets the needs of its intended users. However, as Patton (1997) points out, including stakeholders throughout the evaluation process is often important to avoid surprises when the final report is disseminated. The role defined for the stakeholders needs to fit within the level of funding for the evaluation and, where feasible, allow for ongoing input into the interpretation of results. This helps ensure that the stakeholders do not lose patience with the demands of the evaluation or get bogged down on efforts to define their role (Weiss, 1991).

AEA's *Guiding Principles for Evaluators* (2006) lists four principles specific to stakeholder involvement:

1. Understand, respect, and take into account differences among stakeholders, such as interests, culture, religion, disability, age, sexual orientation, and ethnicity.
2. Include relevant perspectives and interests of the full range of stakeholders.
3. Allow stakeholders access to, and actively disseminate, evaluative information.
4. Maintain a balance between the evaluation sponsor and other stakeholder needs and interests.

It may be most efficient to provide stakeholders with a written description of their roles and expectations when they are invited to participate. People generally appreciate knowing the level of time commitment they are being asked to make, the expectations for their ongoing participation, and how their participation can benefit the program and themselves.

Establish Group Processes for Ongoing Stakeholder Input

Several researchers have developed or established procedures and processes to engage and maintain stakeholder involvement. In 1996, Torres, Preskill, and Pointek reported findings of a survey of AEA members' experiences communicating with stakeholders and identified the following elements of effective communication:

- Ongoing, collaborative communication processes with periodic meetings, informal conversations, memos, and draft reports
- Varied formats of communication (e.g., reports, summaries, verbal presentation, e-mail)
- Information presented in a concise and specific manner using vivid and concrete illustrations

Given how busy most people's lives are, it is critical that the evaluator determine effective ways to communicate with stakeholders both when their concentrated efforts are desired (e.g., review of draft data collection instruments) and when their ongoing involvement is needed (e.g., updates on evaluation progress to maintain interest in the findings).

DESCRIBE THE PROGRAM

It is vital to understand the stage of development of the program to be evaluated and the context within which it is currently operating. After meeting with key stakeholders, the evaluator thoroughly reviews program documents and other literature related to the program and its proposed outcomes. At the same time, the evaluator may interview key staff and program stakeholders to understand the history and evolution of the program, develop logic models or conceptual frameworks to visually depict how the program is thought to function, and create tools that begin to specify the potential issues of interest for the evaluation. Issues to consider during this process, as well as possible tools to use, are discussed below.

Determine Program Theory or Logic

The process of program description has been addressed by many researchers who have suggested developing tools such as logic models or conceptual frameworks. One process, which was developed in the 1970s, is *evaluability assessment*. Evaluability assessment is an analysis of the feasibility and utility of the evaluation (Wholey, 1978). This process was created to determine the extent to which an effectiveness evaluation was feasible for a particular program (Smith, 1989). The evaluator must clarify what the program is intended to accomplish and determine the measurements of program performance that are feasible and relevant for the goals of the evaluation. This involves a review of program documents such as program plans, meeting minutes, proposals, progress reports, attendance records, and other archival information related to the program. Evaluability assessment also requires evaluators to familiarize themselves with the current literature on the issue under study. The goal is to help the evaluator understand the work that has already been done, the stage of development of the program, and the major objectives and activities that are discussed in the program documents.

During this process, the evaluator completes the following tasks:

> Clarifies the logic of the programs (resources, activities, objectives and causal links between activity and objectives); identifies those portions of the program which are ready for useful evaluation (well-defined objectives; plausible, testable causal links between activities and objectives; well-defined uses for evaluation information); and identifies feasible evaluation and management alternatives. (Wholey, 1978, p. 54)

If a program has a logic model, the evaluator would also review it to further clarify program resources and short- and long-term objectives. It is typically during this step that the evaluator develops a draft conceptual framework to examine and explain the relationships that exist among program goals, objectives, and outcomes (CDC, 1999). This information is then collated and integrated to form a conceptual model of the intended processes of the program. Conceptual models or frameworks typically include a figure with circles and arrows to depict how the program is expected to create change. For some programs, it may be useful to create more than one model or framework that depicts different levels of the evaluation. Programs being evaluated for CDC, for example, may best be described with logic models of the local- or state-level program and a conceptual framework of the overall, national aspect of the program. Having models to depict both of these levels can help the evaluator better understand the program and incorporate corresponding processes and outcomes in the overall conceptual framework for the evaluation.

A conceptual framework is generally more theoretically based and conceptual than a logic model. It can be used to conceptualize how variables related to the program go together and should work to create change. A logic model tends to be program specific and provides a more detailed description of the planned activities and outputs of a program. A logic model can also help the evaluator assess program activities and resource allocation. A key advantage of a conceptual framework in evaluation planning is that it identifies the proposed interrelationships across major program phases (e.g., capacity building, partnership and collaboration development) and the expected relationship between these phases and the program's outcomes (e.g., access to services). Often, the evaluation sponsors have a preference as to which type of model they want the evaluator to create. Depending on the stage of development at which the evaluation is to occur, logic models may have already been created and used by staff in organizing the program activities. Both the logic model and conceptual framework can be used as a guide in prioritizing relationships and variables of critical importance and in identifying appropriate measures to incorporate into the evaluation. Wholey (1978) notes that "evaluation is unlikely to be useful unless certain 'evaluation planning standards' are satisfied: (1) Program objectives are well defined, (2) causal links between program activities and objectives are plausible and testable, and (3) intended uses of evaluation information are well defined" (p. 53).

As the framework or model is being crafted and/or refined, the evaluator can also begin to specify evaluation questions of interest by creating an evaluation planning matrix (EPM). Using this matrix, the evaluator can determine domains or areas of interest that could be included in the evaluation plan. These domains may be stated as goals for the program, objectives, or theoretical constructs that include related evaluation questions.

As a tool, the EPM helps to organize the evaluation questions around identified goals or domains. It can also be useful in specifying short- and long-term outcomes of interest, data sources, data elements, and other issues of interest to the evaluator and stakeholders.

A typical EPM might begin with the left-hand column specifying the evaluation questions under study. These are generally organized around the domains or goals that are specified as the most important to assess. When the evaluator first begins drafting the EPM, the list of questions should be all-inclusive, incorporating feedback from the sponsor, staff, and stakeholders, so that this thorough document can be used as a guide when the process of focusing the evaluation begins. Evaluation questions at this stage can be descriptive (e.g., "What activities are the program engaged in?") or more proscriptive in terms of identifying outcomes (e.g., "What are the actual versus projected costs of completing each activity?").

Understand Program History and Evolution

As the evaluator is becoming immersed in describing the program, features that need to be understood include its history and evolution, including understanding the stage of program development for which the evaluation is to occur. As described earlier, new programs will require different types of outcomes and methods than older, more established programs where long-term outcomes are expected to be assessed.

As a tool like the EPM is created, the evaluator should also specify each type of outcome of interest, which is driven in part by the stage of program development to be measured. Different terms from the literature to depict outcomes include *process,* or *formative,* for outcomes that can be measured early in program development (i.e., short-term outcomes); *summative, effectiveness,* or *impact* for outcomes that can be assessed within the first few years of program implementation (i.e., intermediate outcomes); or *long-term* for outcomes that are assessed over the course of the evaluation. However, many of the terms often do not resonate with the evaluation sponsor or stakeholders and are difficult to understand; thus, the evaluator will need to use consistent language so that there is a common understanding of the types of outcomes to be included in the plan.

It is also important for the evaluator to work with the sponsor and others to specify to which time period each refers, because this can depend on several factors, including the stage of program development, the length of time the program will be in existence, the focus of the program, or the theoretical framework guiding the program and evaluation. For example, a new program that will be in existence for 5 years may have short-term, intermediate, and long-term outcomes. However, an evaluation that occurs in a program's last year and relies on no baseline measures may have only short-term and possibly intermediate outcomes. A program that is likely to have a delayed effect, such as training physicians in a new clinical practice, may have limited short-term effects on patient outcomes but more sustained long-term effects. Similarly, if a program's logic model focuses on intermediate outcomes, it may not be necessary to incorporate measures of long-term effects into the evaluation plan. Table 2.3 describes the three primary types of outcomes to incorporate into an evaluation plan.

As questions and outcomes are being specified, clarified, and streamlined, the evaluator needs to identify available data sources and develop plans to collect data that are not otherwise available. By specifying in the EPM which evaluation outcomes already have available data sources, the evaluator can quickly identify gaps in the required data. Depending on the specificity of the EPM, the evaluator also can begin to determine the data elements that need to be collected to answer the questions, either from

Table 2.3   Types of Outcomes

Type of Outcome	Description of Outcome
Short-term or process (also referred to as formative)	Measures specific to each evaluation question assessed within the first year of program implementation: Short-term measures are typically formative in nature with a focus on the process of program implementation.
Intermediate or effectiveness (also referred to as summative or impact)	Measures specific to each evaluation question assessed within the first few years of program implementation: Intermediate outcomes are typically related to behavior or policy change, with a focus on the direct or indirect effects of the program on participants, as well as larger systems and possibly the community (Patton, 1997).
Long-term	Measures specific to each evaluation question assessed over the course of the evaluation to determine the extent to which the activities have resulted in long-term change. Depending on the time allotted for the evaluation, long-term outcomes may not be feasible to include in the design. In evaluation research, many researchers term these simply as outcome evaluation, meaning the extent to which desired outcomes are being achieved (Patton, 1997).

existing data sources or through data to be collected in the evaluation. The data elements reflect the actual data variables or indicators used to assess the corresponding outcome. For instance, to evaluate who received services through a program, the evaluator may specify that demographic variables of the individuals served need to be collected.

An EPM of activities, outcomes, and data sources is a useful organizational tool that flows from the conceptual framework. As the evaluator gains expertise in the program under study, he or she will be more adept at determining which evaluation questions seem feasible to measure and which will be of the greatest importance or usefulness to the stakeholders. This expertise also will help the evaluator determine what is feasible given the budget allocated for the evaluation.

FOCUS THE EVALUATION

The evaluation must be focused to assess the issues of greatest importance to stakeholders, given the available resources dedicated to evaluation and surveillance (CDC, 1999). At this point in the evaluation planning process, the evaluator has created a long list of potential evaluation questions that have been obtained through ongoing input from stakeholders, through review of program documents, and by describing each aspect of the program to be evaluated. The following subsections describe issues to address when focusing the evaluation.

Complete Comprehensive List of Evaluation Questions

To focus the evaluation, the evaluator needs to work with the sponsor to prioritize needs to address in the evaluation plan. In meeting with the sponsor, the evaluator should determine if the list of potential evaluation questions to include in the final plan is complete. During this step, additional stakeholders often need to be engaged to help further refine the evaluation objectives. As stakeholders are included, the evaluator needs to be able to conduct a variety of group processes to build consensus as to which evaluation questions are of the greatest importance and also feasible to measure. Reducing mortality rates from lung cancer may be an ultimate goal of a tobacco cessation program, but this is unlikely to happen in the evaluation period and would be difficult to attribute to the program even if a reduction were found. Therefore, the evaluator needs to help the stakeholders understand the limits of evaluation so that there are realistic expectations as to which questions an evaluation study can answer. The evaluator must also provide leadership in determining the data and measures to be used given the evaluation goals and available resources. To this end, the evaluator may want to share the EPM with the stakeholders as an organizing tool for discussion.

Ensure Feasibility

As the evaluator creates the EPM or a similar tool to guide the planning process, work can be done with the stakeholders to determine which outcomes can feasibly be addressed within the scope of the planned evaluation. As noted by Rossi et al. (2004),

> Good evaluation questions must first of all be reasonable and appropriate. That is, they must identify performance dimensions that are relevant to the expectations stakeholders hold for the program and that represent domains in which the program can realistically hope to have accomplishments. (p. 70)

However, as Patton (1997) notes, "No evaluation can answer all potential questions equally well. This means that some process is necessary for narrowing the ranges of possible questions to focus the evaluation" (p. 42). This process needs to incorporate strategies for including all questions that should be included and excluding any questions that are less important or cannot be measured feasibly within the scope of the evaluation.

One aspect of feasibility that is not always considered is the burden that potential data collection can impose on the people implementing the program. In many situations, the assessment of burden needs to be at the forefront in the evaluator's rationale for suggesting the inclusion or elimination of certain evaluation questions. One such example would be if the evaluation sponsor were a national organization and the purpose of the evaluation were to understand the processes and outcomes of a program being implemented at the local level. In this scenario, each evaluation question would likely require some type of data collection at the local level. Therefore, if the evaluation questions were to include the domains of program cost-effectiveness, delivery of adequate and timely services to patients, and program management, this array of issues would translate into a great deal of data that local programs would be responsible for collecting and providing to the evaluator. If the local programs were to receive little or no funding to assist with the program evaluation, then this issue would need to be discussed with the program stakeholders and sponsors so that they would understand what the programs were being asked to do. In some situations the evaluator needs to push this issue, because without some concession to reduce the burden the quality of the data provided will be limited and the resulting evaluation will be compromised.

Prioritize Questions to Answer

Each step in the planning process builds to this point of refining the evaluation questions. The more stakeholders who have been involved throughout the planning process and the more developed a program is, the more evaluation questions there are likely to be. It then becomes the evaluator's task to work with stakeholders to prioritize questions that are feasible to answer and likely to provide valid answers. As noted by Rossi et al. (2004),

> The evaluator who thoroughly explores stakeholder concerns and conducts an analysis of program issues guided by carefully developed descriptions of program theory will turn up many questions that the evaluation might address. The task at this point becomes one of organizing questions according to distinct themes and setting priorities among them. (p. 96)

This process of organizing questions around themes is similar to developing an EPM. This organization helps lay out the evaluation questions and possible outcomes and serves as a foundation for identifying both the questions that can and should be answered through the evaluation and those that are either infeasible or impractical to ask. Rossi et al. (2004) discuss an evaluation hierarchy of questions that include assessments of the following:

- Need for the program
- Program design and theory
- Program process and implementation
- Program outcome
- Program costs and efficiency

Though these types of questions may be important to answer, some may not be of the greatest priority to the sponsors and stakeholders. Rossi et al. (2004) note that "for an evaluation question to be answerable, it must be possible to identify some evidence or 'observables' that can realistically be obtained and that will be credible as the basis for an answer" (p. 72). The evaluator needs to assess each question to determine if data sources for answering it are available or if the available resources allow for collection of those data sources. The collection of cost data from program staff, for example, can be quite burdensome and time consuming. Depending on the type of program, the data that need to be collected can be quite complex. Much of these data, such as procedure codes for services provided to a patient in order to know the reimbursement rate for those services, are not elements that a program would necessarily plan to gather or have access to. First, decisions will need to be made to determine what the stakeholders hope to get out of the evaluation and which questions in the planning tool can be answered.

Once the determination is made that certain questions can be answered through available or gathered data, the evaluator needs to facilitate group processes with the sponsors and stakeholders to ensure that stakeholders are afforded the opportunity to provide direction. Patton (1997) provides a number of "alternative ways of focusing evaluations" that can assist an evaluator in determining how to best facilitate this process (p. 192). At this point in the process, the evaluator can use the information about the purpose of the evaluation, the context within which it is to be conducted, and the level of the evaluation to refine the evaluation questions. If the evaluation is to focus on understanding program implementation and the extent to which there is fidelity to the program design, then questions related to outcomes such as changes in health-related measures (e.g., decreased blood pressure) may not be of importance and may need to be put aside in the evaluation planning. Often the evaluator is engaging in a long-term evaluation over a number of years, in which case the evaluator can inform stakeholders that the evaluation planning process can be revisited at specific points in time in order to add additional evaluation questions if resources are available. As Stake (1991) notes, "We cannot know all important questions at the start of evaluation, so we need a means to discover important questions that are not apparent initially" (p. 281). The evaluator needs to build in a process for reassessing the evaluation plan over time and as lessons are learned.

As decisions are made about which questions to include in the evaluation plan, the evaluator needs to remain neutral and objective but also understand the issues that are important to stakeholders (Chelimsky, 1995). During the process of prioritizing, it is important for the evaluator to recognize and discuss with stakeholders the fact that "focusing an evaluation is an interactive process between evaluators and the primary intended users of the evaluation. It can be a difficult process because deciding what will be evaluated means deciding what will not be evaluated" (Patton, 1997, p. 189). Ultimately, the evaluator needs to be prepared to guide the stakeholders, and particularly the evaluation sponsor, to understand what can feasibly be done within the scope of the evaluation. Sponsors often believe that all their answers can be addressed in an evaluation, no matter how broad their questions and how small the project's funding. In focusing the evaluation, the evaluator needs to help people understand what an evaluation entails, the questions the evaluation can answer, and the types of resources that would be needed to answer particular questions. The evaluator also needs to be clear about the limitations of an evaluation and the effect the budget for an evaluation can have on its design.

CONCLUSION

- Evaluation planning is a process that involves five steps guided by the evaluator: (1) assessing the context, (2) gathering reconnaissance, (3) engaging stakeholders, (4) describing the program, and (5) focusing the evaluation.
- Each step includes issues that need to be proactively considered and discussed with the evaluation stakeholders and sponsor.
- Before developing an evaluation plan, the evaluator needs to assess the context and gather reconnaissance about the program and the environment within which the evaluation is to be conducted, including the following:
  - Understanding the organizational and political environment, including the stage of development of the program
  - Defining the relationship between the evaluator and the evaluation sponsor
  - Determining the level of the program evaluation
  - Specifying the uses of the evaluation findings
  - Validating the stakeholders' perspectives
- When engaging stakeholders, it is important for the evaluator to include as many individuals and organizations as possible in the planning process, given the level of resources and time required to facilitate stakeholder processes, and ensuring that the evaluation can afford their ongoing engagement.
- Engaging stakeholders should involve clearly defining their roles and the ongoing expectations for their involvement, and it should include a plan for effective communication over time. Time and funding constraints are important to consider in defining stakeholder roles and involvement because this work can be very time and labor intensive.
- The evaluator can use many resources for describing the program, including published and extant literature, all program documentation, and interviews with staff and stakeholders.
- Tools such as logic models, conceptual frameworks, and EPMs can be developed to provide guidance throughout the evaluation planning process and during implementation.
- Focusing the evaluation is an iterative process that requires the evaluator to serve as facilitator and trainer. Group processes have to be facilitated to allow

stakeholders the opportunity to provide input into which questions are to be addressed in the evaluation.

• The evaluator needs to consider each evaluation question in terms of how feasible it is to answer, the burden that data collection would impose on others who may not have the staff or expertise to provide it, and the use of the data to be collected to inform the evaluation. With stakeholder and sponsor input, the evaluator needs to make tough choices about which questions can be addressed within the scope and resources of the evaluation.

• The evaluator needs to educate the stakeholders (including sponsors) about the strengths and limitations of the evaluation in general and the feasibility of different designs for the particular program.

REFERENCES

American Evaluation Association. (2006). *Guiding principles for evaluators.* Retrieved January 25, 2007, from http://www.eval.org/GPTraining/GP%20 Training%20Final/gp.principles.pdf

Bamberger, M., Rugh, J., & Mabry, L. (2006). *Real world evaluation: Working under budget, time, data, and political constraints.* Thousand Oaks, CA: Sage.

Centers for Disease Control and Prevention. (1999). Framework for program evaluation in public health. *Morbidity and Mortality Weekly Report, 48*(RR11), 1–40.

Chelimsky, E. (1995, November). *The political environment of evaluation and what it means for the development of the field.* American Evaluation Association Presidential Address, Vancouver, Canada. *Evaluation Practice, 16*(3), 215–225.

Cronbach, L. J. (1982). *Designing evaluations of educational and social programs.* San Francisco: Jossey-Bass.

Cronbach, L. J. (1991). Functional evaluation design for a world of political accommodation. In W. R. Shadish, T. D. Cook, & L. C. Leviton (Eds.), *Foundations of program evaluation: Theories of practice* (pp. 323–376). Thousand Oaks, CA: Sage.

Joint Committee on Standards for Educational Evaluation. (1994). *The program evaluation standards.* Thousand Oaks, CA: Sage.

Patton, M. (1997). *Utilization focused evaluation: The new century text.* Thousand Oaks, CA: Sage.

Reineke, R. A. (1991). Stakeholder involvement in evaluation: Suggestions for practice. *Evaluation Practice, 12*(1), 39–44.

Rossi, P. H., Lipsey, M. W., & Freeman, H. E. (2004). *Evaluation: A systematic approach* (7th ed.). Thousand Oaks, CA: Sage.

Smith, M. F. (1989). *Evaluability assessment: A practical approach.* Boston: Kluwer Academic.

Stake, R. E. (1991). Responsive evaluation and qualitative methods. In W. R. Shadish, T. D. Cook, & L. C. Leviton (Eds.), *Foundations of program evaluation: Theories of practice* (pp. 270–314). Thousand Oaks, CA: Sage.

Torres, R. T., Preskill, H. S., & Pointek, M. E. (1996). *Evaluation strategies for community and reporting: Enhancing learning in organizations.* Thousand Oaks, CA: Sage.

Weiss, C. H. (1973). The politics of impact measurement. *Policy Studies Journal, 1,* 37–45.

Weiss, C. H. (1991). Linking evaluation to policy research. In W. R. Shadish, T. D. Cook, & L. C. Leviton (Eds.), *Foundations of program evaluation: Theories of practice* (pp. 179–224). Thousand Oaks, CA: Sage.

Wholey, J. S. (1978). *Zero-base budgeting and program evaluation.* Washington, DC: Lexington Books.

3

PLANNING FOR AN EDUCATION EVALUATION

Julie A. Marshall

A thorough analysis of contextual factors in the school setting can help inform and clarify the evaluation questions that are most meaningful and the design and assessment methods that are most feasible. The importance of specific contextual factors may differ from one program evaluation to another, depending on individuals in the school setting and the surrounding community (e.g., their values and leadership style), existing policies, local decision-making and policymaking structures, and economic factors. This chapter describes the contextual factors that we identified as important, and how they were handled, in planning the evaluation of a school-based nutrition curriculum in a rural, low-income community.

BACKGROUND ON EDUCATION EVALUATION

The Integrated Nutrition Education Program (INEP) was developed by education and nutrition specialists in Denver for elementary-aged children (Auld, Romaniello, Heimendinger, Hambidge, & Hambidge, 1998, 1999). In the 2007–2008 school year, lessons were being taught in 805 classes, 64 schools, and 12 districts reaching approximately 22,000 students in urban and rural Colorado. The lessons integrate nutrition concepts into the core curriculum of math, science, literacy, and social studies. As part of the lessons, students practice hands-on food preparation, tasting, and cooperative learning. Activities are not only fun, but they are designed to build skills and confidence in academic areas. For example, in one lesson, second-grade students taste different types of apples and then use sticky notes to create (on a wall or blackboard) a histogram of student preferences for each type of apple. The lesson is accompanied by a short story and discussion that builds literacy skills while linking the apple tasting to dietary guidelines that recommend eating at least five fruits and vegetables a day.

Curriculum development began in 1993 as a result of the recognized link between diet in childhood and chronic disease later in life, increasingly limited opportunities for children to taste and prepare healthy foods, and the lack of school-based nutrition education in elementary schools. By 1998, the curriculum was being implemented in 50 K–5 classrooms in four schools within the Denver public school system. The program included trained resource teachers conducting lessons with the support of the classroom teacher, in part to provide teachers with experiential training in the classroom setting. This approach was designed to build teachers' knowledge, skills, and confidence so they would be prepared to deliver the lessons independently. For sustainability, the curriculum was funded through the Food Stamp Nutrition Education (FSNE) program, which allowed teacher time and resources devoted to nutrition education in low-income schools to count toward matching funds from the U.S. Department of Agriculture (USDA). In these early years, evaluations assessing plate waste in school lunchrooms consistently found that children who received the curriculum ate 0.4 more servings of fruits and vegetables in the lunchroom than children who did not. Evaluations also found that children in the program self-reported greater increases in knowledge and self-efficacy regarding food preparation and consumption of fruits and vegetables than students in comparison classrooms (Auld et al., 1998).

In 1998, the Rocky Mountain Prevention Research Center (RMPRC) collaborated with the curriculum developers to incorporate local foods and test curriculum effectiveness in a rural school district. Beginning in 2000, a cohort of about 200 students received the curriculum in second and third grades from a local resource teacher trained by the Denver-based INEP. Students who received the 28 lessons in each grade were found to have more positive attitudes and greater knowledge about healthy eating and physical activity than students who did not receive the lessons. They also felt more confident in their ability to eat healthy foods and engage in healthy physical activities (Belansky et al., 2006).

The evaluation planning described in this chapter occurred as a result of recommendations made by the RMPRC Community Advisory Board (CAB) early in 2003. CAB included representatives from health, education, and government in the same rural community where INEP had been implemented and tested. CAB members who had personal experience with the curriculum included the school district's health coordinator, a parent, and a school board member. CAB concluded that the first priority of RMPRC in the next funding cycle should be to study an environmental approach to influence health behavior in schools. They also felt that the prior investment in INEP merited long-term follow-up to determine its impact on children and to understand the adoption of the program among second- and third-grade teachers, but they advised that we commit minimal resources to the follow-up evaluation of the curriculum.

From 2002 to date, the INEP curriculum has been available for second- and third-grade teachers in this rural district to use on a voluntary basis. RMPRC and the Denver-based INEP have continued to provide support (equipment, purchase of foods, and revised curriculum notebooks) to classroom teachers who choose to teach the lessons. In fall 2007, the program was expanded to include kindergarten, first, fourth, and fifth grades in two other schools in the district. Children who initially received the lessons in second and third grade (2000–2002) were now in ninth grade. The information provided here has been organized using the Evaluation Planning Incorporating Context (EPIC) model to provide examples of what to consider when planning an evaluation within a school setting. However, the process did not occur with explicit attention to each issue considered or as a linear progression from evaluation planning to implementation. For example, although some contextual factors were known from previous work, a better understanding evolved as the project team worked through the development of data collection tools and the analysis that occurred each year during the evaluation.

ASSESS CONTEXT

Understand the Organizational and Political Environment

Organizational Structure

Even brief collaborations can help in developing relationships with partners that can be built on in the future. In 1993, I was involved in a collaborative grant proposal that did not end up being funded but that turned out to be the stimulus for developing INEP. INEP evolved as a partnership with faculty in the Department of Pediatrics at the University of Colorado, Denver, and the headmaster and staff at Stanley British Primary School; faculty from the Department of Food Science and Human Nutrition at Colorado State University provided evaluation support. Because the senior faculty member was open to as-yet undefined possibilities for the program, he invited me to attend meetings periodically that kept me informed and later helped me understand some of the developmental stages, organizational structure, and financial support for INEP. The organizational structure and funding described in this section are potential determinants of the curriculum's evolution, implementation, and sustainability. As part of the evaluation planning process, the evaluator has to determine the focus of the evaluation, which can include any of these features.

INEP is embedded in two organizational structures. It is centrally administered by staff in the Department of Pediatrics in the School of Medicine at the University of Colorado, Denver, with funds from the USDA FSNE program that flow through Colorado State University. The program is supported with state funds only to the extent that these nonfederal funds support nutrition education in low-income schools and qualify as matching dollars for funds coming from USDA. In the initial phase of adapting and testing the curriculum with stakeholders in this rural community (1999–2002), RMPRC housed the INEP resource teacher and provided staff support for related parent events and evaluation activities. After 2002, RMPRC research staff continued to provide support to classroom teachers with funding from USDA. This support included food shopping, basic preparation of foods, and organization of bins for each teacher with cooking equipment, books, and other materials needed during the lesson and for clean-up afterward. Ongoing evaluation was conducted with RMPRC core funding from the Centers for Disease Control and Prevention (CDC).

INEP implementation occurs within the public school system. The organizational structure of a school system is typically hierarchical, with elementary students assigned to a teacher's classroom, teachers reporting to a school principal, and principals reporting to a district superintendent, who reports directly to the local school board. Because the superintendent is hired (and can be fired) by the board, it can be an extremely political position. In addition to their local school board, superintendents also report to the state Board of Education; a district superintendent may be responsible for hundreds of reports that go to the state board, and smaller districts may not have sufficient staff for delegation of this work. The state board in turn reports to several agencies at the federal level including the Department of Education and USDA, where the school lunch program is housed. State agencies provide guidance and expertise to school districts and may act as intermediaries to ensure compliance with federal regulations.

This rural extension of INEP was initially housed in a single school building with 350 to 400 students in a school district of about 2,300 students.

The principal made a classroom available exclusively for the nutrition lessons, which provided some visibility and explicit support for the program within the school. However, at the district level, the visibility of the program in 2002 was limited except to the extent that children brought home recipes and began to ask for items like fruits and vegetables that they had prepared in the classroom. The school district health coordinator was a member of RMPRC CAB and had been a second-grade teacher in the same school where INEP lessons were conducted. She provided an important link to the district administration until her position was eliminated in 2007 due to district restructuring aimed at improving standardized test scores. In 2005, we invited the district wellness committee to observe INEP lessons being delivered at the school during the time when the committee was developing the district's federally mandated school wellness policy. Observing the lessons brings INEP to life more effectively than listening to a description of the program or reviewing the written documentation. During the lessons, children actively work together; they are engaged in the learning process and have fun preparing and tasting foods. The superintendent attended class to observe the lessons in action. In 2007, expansion of the program to other schools in the district was negotiated with school principals who then sought input from teachers and staff on whether to adopt the curriculum in each school.

Buy-in is important at multiple levels, and what is important to administrators may differ from what is important to teachers. We recently presented a new project to the superintendent and principals in the same school district in which the case study was conducted, and the superintendent explained that his explicit criteria for considering any new program were that the program be transparent (i.e., that it have no hidden agendas), efficient, effective, and improve what was already being done in the district. For teachers, buy-in was related to somewhat different factors: the perceived value of the lessons; the time and logistical issues required in lesson preparation, implementation, and clean-up; and whether the lessons enhanced other activities in their classroom. These different perspectives must be addressed when obtaining buy-in (see "Lessons Learned" No. 1 later in this chapter).

Stage of Development

From 1999 to 2002, INEP was implemented for the first time in a rural setting 200 miles from the Denver-based administrative offices. An outcome evaluation (Belansky et al., 2006) was conducted to determine if knowledge and attitude changes were similar to results previously reported in Denver schools. The subsequent evaluation (2003–2009) had two components:

1. *Long-term curriculum outcomes in students.* Follow-up of students through middle school extended the earlier outcome evaluation to determine if differences in knowledge and attitudes persisted over time when students who received the curriculum were compared with a cohort 1 year older who did not receive the curriculum. An outcome evaluation usually requires a quantitative analysis with sufficient precision to detect meaningful group differences. During the evaluation planning process, we had to define the measurable outcome objectives expected of students 2 to 5 years after the curriculum was delivered. In second grade, students were 7 or 8 years old, and by eighth grade they were 13 or 14 years old. The measurement methods needed to be valid and reliable at each age. From a logistical perspective, the fact that course schedules in middle school vary by student and across the day (unlike in elementary school) makes it more difficult to identify a single class for survey administration.

2. *Adoption of the curriculum among second- and third-grade teachers.* Here the primary objective was to understand how the curriculum was being implemented and adapted by teachers (in contrast to the outcome evaluation that focused on students). We were interested in teacher perspectives on barriers and facilitators for administering the curriculum to inform adaptations or modifications for future implementation and long-term sustainability. We tracked which lessons were taught by which teachers and systematically surveyed teachers after each lesson to quantitatively understand curriculum adaptation and delivery. Because the curriculum was voluntary, we could ask questions in key informant interviews to understand teacher perspectives on what factors influenced whether they chose to use the lessons in their classrooms.

Current Sociopolitical Environment

Policies governing schools may come from local, district, state, or federal levels; they vary by state and by the size of the school district. School policy may also be influenced by members of the administrative staff within a district and school building, the school board, parents, and the community surrounding the school. In large school districts, we have found that a written application and approval from a districtwide committee is often required for research or evaluation projects. School-level staff are not always aware of this process and may provide verbal approval that later requires district approval. In large districts, there may be more than one committee (e.g., a program committee and a research committee), and the lines are not always clear as to where a particular evaluation belongs because most new programs also have an evaluation component. If committee approval is required, it can take months to obtain, so the application process should be started well before activities in the school are scheduled to begin. In both large and small districts, we have found that building a good personal relationship with the superintendent or principal is critical. In small districts, people see each other on a regular basis (e.g., in the grocery store). Board members may be very influential as well as responsive to community members they know personally. In small districts, I have been advised to have a conversation with the superintendent at the outset about the local climate. Most superintendents in small districts are open to this type of conversation. Asking about the school board and school principals helps to better understand the political environment and to determine whether they would be receptive to the program or evaluation being planned.

At the school and district levels, we have had one RMPRC staff member from the community working with school staff since 1999. This staff continuity makes it easier to maintain relationships. If there is turnover in the evaluation staff, it is important to introduce new members to all staff in the building. Our staff member is always upbeat and reliable, and she values the personal relationships with the school staff. She considers their needs and the importance of being a team player, whether dealing with the principal, secretaries, classroom teachers, or janitors who facilitate set-up and clean-up of the "nutrition room."

In Colorado, there is a strong belief in local control. The state board of education provides guidance on grade-level standards in core content areas, but local school districts are responsible for developing a plan to meet those standards. For example, in 2007, Colorado was the only state without legislation on minimum requirements for physical education. The assumption is that local school districts are in the best position to establish these policies (see "Lessons Learned" No. 4). Local decisions may be made either primarily by the superintendent and then handed down to the principal or primarily by the principal who then informs the superintendent. The level of input from teachers in the decision-making process also varies depending on the local school administration.

At the same time, local-level decisions are often driven by federal mandates such as No Child Left Behind, which is tied to school funding, or the requirement to establish a local school wellness policy by July 2006, which was not tied to funding; USDA regulations for free and reduced-cost lunch and breakfast programs; and Title I, which provides supplementary funding in schools with a high proportion of children from low-income homes. Substantial federal funds come into low-income schools through these mechanisms, and mandates tied to those funds usually have major implications for the school district and are thus taken seriously.

Several important factors, which are probably not unique to our study communities, need to be considered in implementing and evaluating health programs in the school setting:

- High-stakes testing
- Poverty
- The increasing burden on America's schools

High-Stakes Testing

The Colorado Standardized Assessment Program (CSAP) began in 1997, 5 years before the federally mandated No Child Left Behind policy went into effect. CSAP became Colorado's measurement tool for the federal policy. In addition to assessing and providing feedback to students and parents about individual student proficiency in mathematics, reading and writing, and science in 3rd through 10th grades, the program uses aggregate data by school as the primary measure of school performance. Numerous federal grant programs are tied to this performance measure. For example, if a school does not meet specified levels of performance for 2 consecutive years, it is required to create a school improvement plan to maintain Title 1 funding. Any school with three consecutive unsatisfactory ratings is converted into a charter school. A school district can lose its accreditation by having consistently low-scoring schools.

CSAPs are one of the first barriers mentioned when considering any program or evaluation that may compete for resources that would otherwise be devoted to academic instruction, including teacher or student time during the school day. We have observed stress among teachers who seemed to be directly linked to the climate created by high-stakes testing. Some teachers expressed concerns that the high-stakes testing environment discourages teacher creativity and that the increased demands placed on teachers make it difficult for them to find time to communicate with and learn from each other. It has always been a priority of INEP to minimize any INEP-related burden on teachers so that the curriculum supports, rather than competes with, other academic activities or resources. This concern has been addressed in multiple ways. First, the INEP curriculum is designed to address core academic content areas. When we began our collaboration in 1999, we asked school staff which content areas they would like the lessons to emphasize. They specified that they wanted literacy and math to be the primary academic foci of the lessons. Over time, the curriculum manual has been enhanced so that the state standards in core content areas are explicitly linked to components of the lessons. Second, school resources devoted to the curriculum, even for oversight, have been minimal. INEP includes a teacher manual that provides easy-to-follow step-by-step instructions, separate lists of required materials, concise background on the topic, and one-page summary sheets that teachers can refer to during the lessons. The program also provides all materials and funds and supervises a staff person who does the grocery shopping and packages foods needed by each teacher for the lessons.

Process evaluation during initial implementation and in our studies of adoption helped us understand how to achieve these goals and provided estimates of the amount of teacher time required to prepare and deliver the lessons. In planning the long-term outcome evaluation for students, the project team noted that there is evidence that students do better on the writing component of the CSAP test if they practice in advance. This led to the development of a seventh-grade writing assessment that gave students practice in writing a response to a CSAP-style open-ended question. For INEP evaluation purposes, content analysis of the essays was used to assess the depth and accuracy of the students' knowledge and their ability to apply the concepts of INEP.

Informal evaluation by the INEP administrative staff looking at CSAP scores across the state in schools implementing INEP saw gains in CSAP scores comparable to schools without INEP. Conducting a systematic assessment of CSAP scores before and after introduction of INEP and then comparing this to the change in CSAP scores at comparable schools not receiving INEP is an example of identifying an evaluation question that addresses important adoption and sustainability issues for those responsible for making decisions about committing resources and time to the program.

Poverty

Because INEP has been funded through the USDA FSNE program, school eligibility is based on the percentage of children in the school eligible for free or reduced-cost lunch. Materials are available to nonqualifying schools, but those schools must fund and administer the program themselves.

The rural area where we work includes several of the poorest counties in the state, and all districts qualify for INEP. In this low-income context, most children are less prepared when entering school and may have less support to succeed academically than their higher-income counterparts. In ethnographic studies with families of young children in this community (Brett, Heimendinger, Boender, Morin, & Marshall, 2002), it was common to find two-parent and single-parent working families. When all adult members of the family are working, there are often scheduling conflicts, making time together as a family infrequent and unpredictable. Young children may have insufficient parental support for basic self-care or they may have to care for younger siblings, leaving little time for school work. The resulting challenges and stress experienced by teachers in these schools appear to be exacerbated by the high-stakes testing described above. Understanding how poverty affects the lives of children and school staff may inform evaluation questions and related measures.

Personally and professionally, an invaluable outcome of having teachers participate in the project team came from the insight they provided into the lives of these children, as well as their own struggles and stress as dedicated teachers. One teacher thought that the INEP lessons might be enough to influence a child to put milk in a younger sibling's bottle instead of Kool-Aid. Some children do not have food outside of school near the end of the month, and thus the food from INEP lessons sometimes doubled as a healthy snack within the classroom setting. This type of contextual knowledge and understanding can help inform what degree of "success" can be expected of a program. This knowledge can also inform evaluation questions and measures that may be important to those making policy decisions for disadvantaged populations.

The Increasing Burden on America's Schools

Jamie Vollmer (Vollmer and Associates, 2001) has described the increasingly unrealistic burden that has been placed on schools over the past century. Vollmer's decade-by-decade list includes more than 50 topics, starting in the early 1900s with nutrition and immunizations and expanding by the 1990s to include Internet training, HIV/AIDS education, school-to-work programs, and safety issues ranging from bicycle safety to gun safety. In the first decade of the 21st century, high-stakes testing has been added to these school responsibilities, yet, in most places, no additional time has been added to the school calendar in the past 50 years. This is important contextual information for anyone asking schools to allocate staff time or school resources for curriculum evaluation, which is yet another request that does not directly address the core content standards that schools are mandated to have their students achieve. Recognition of school priorities and the burden placed on schools to address other health-related topics led us to plan evaluation components that would document how often the curriculum addressed core content standards.

The following resources may be helpful background in understanding the sociopolitical context of schools:

• *The 90/90/90 Schools: A Case Study* (Reeves, 2000) describes common classroom strategies in schools with a high percentage of low-income and ethnic minority families and a high percentage of students meeting or achieving high academic standards. Sometimes this research is used by policymakers to dismiss poverty as an excuse for low-performing schools. Instead, the author submits that poverty is relevant to student achievement but that it is not an exclusive determinant of it. Understanding this type of research and how it is being used by policymakers may help in formulating evaluation questions that will be meaningful and used in the policy arena.

• The "value-added" model (Sanders, Saxton, & Horn, 1997; Stone, 1999) is designed to measure the influence that school systems, schools, and teachers have on the academic progress of students. In Colorado, a system is being developed that will track students and teachers over time with a personal identification number for value-added analysis.

• School districts may have their school accountability reports or improvement plans available on the district Web site. Though these reports cannot substitute for personal discussions and observation in the school setting, they may provide a starting place to understand the priorities and decision-making structure of the district.

Define the Relationship Between the Evaluator and the Sponsor

The RMPRC INEP evaluation that started in 2002 was a collaborative evaluation planned and conducted by a project team composed of three to four teachers, a curriculum specialist, a school nurse, the program director from the Denver-based INEP, two researchers, and two part-time research staff. I was the project leader and also responsible for the grant funding the evaluation. The evaluation was funded by CDC but commissioned by the RMPRC CAB.

The primary reason to consider the relationship between the evaluator and the sponsor is to be aware of factors that could compromise study validity. Potential bias could result from a lack of understanding of contextual factors that influence study outcomes or from a lack of objectivity in study design, measurement, or interpretation. CAB members and project team members all believed the curriculum had value, and they wanted to build evidence that would convince the administration to continue its use. Though project team members always acted with integrity, they were invested in the success of the curriculum, and it would have enhanced the evaluation to have a small external advisory committee review the work in depth at least once a year to provide objective expert opinion on study design, analysis, and interpretation.

In addition, the act of preparing for an external review provides an opportunity to step back, assess the progress of the project, and be prepared to address reviewer questions. We have found this to be extremely helpful in other projects. Inevitably, through this process we identify areas that need more careful monitoring, or we can refine questions or additional data collection or documentation that will make the work more meaningful. In the absence of an external advisory committee, RMPRC is visited by three national advisors each year who review progress and results of all center projects. The national advisors were helpful for general direction on INEP, but the review was probably not in sufficient depth for reviewers to identify subtle problems in methodology or unintended bias in interpretation. The time and resources to conduct an external review may not be available for small-scale program evaluations conducted over a short time frame.

Another safety net for our evaluation was that the project team included teachers who had been involved in teaching the curriculum. They could provide insight into whether methods and results were consistent with their actual classroom experience.

Determine the Level of the Evaluation

The two evaluation components were directed at different levels. The perspective of greatest importance in the student follow-up component was related to how the curriculum had influenced students' behavioral determinants (e.g., knowledge, skills, confidence) and behavioral outcomes (e.g., fruit and vegetable consumption) (i.e., individual-level evaluation). On the other hand, in evaluating curriculum adoption among the teachers, we were interested in how and why teachers were implementing the curriculum (i.e., program-level evaluation). Evaluating multiple aspects of an intervention can create some confusion if the components are not clearly distinguished, but this was not a problem for us. A project team meeting might address one or both components. We always started each discussion by reiterating the study question and ensuring that all team members were familiar with the component we would be discussing. This helped ensure that our evaluation design and measures addressed the appropriate questions.

GATHER RECONNAISSANCE

Specify Evaluation Uses

The explicit goal of the evaluation was to refine understanding of curriculum effectiveness and factors that influence curriculum delivery. The intent was to generate knowledge that would be useful in sustaining the curriculum locally and informing curriculum development and delivery in the broader field of health education.

One principle of a more traditional research paradigm is to avoid the situation where the research (or evaluation) process becomes an intervention in and of itself. Instead, the goal is to observe and measure without altering the underlying processes being studied. However, the project team quickly faced a conundrum with respect to the evaluation component assessing curriculum delivery. How much could the project team influence the course of adoption and at the same time study the natural history and factors influencing adoption? Our external advisors suggested that we make ultimate program sustainability our top priority and document how it was achieved rather than maintaining strictly an observer role. This dilemma is common for traditional researchers who transition to more participatory methods that involve the participants being studied in the research process. There is increasing interest in connecting continuous quality improvement and practice-based research, and literature in this area may provide guidance on conducting action-oriented research that produces more generalizable knowledge.

Validate Perspectives

Validating perspectives was not an explicit step of this evaluation except to the extent that local partners recommended that the evaluation be conducted and community members agreed to participate on the project team. To ensure that the evaluation findings would be used, it would have been helpful to interview key stakeholders (e.g., parents, principals, and superintendents) in addition to teachers to determine what information they needed to support adoption of the curriculum.

ENGAGE STAKEHOLDERS

Identify and Invite Stakeholders

An initial planning group for the study included one Denver-based researcher, three research staff from the community, and the school district health coordinator. This group defined a process for identifying teachers to participate as project team members. All teachers received an invitation in their school mailbox briefly describing the project, the team composition, their role, the time commitment, compensation, and qualifications. Qualifications consisted of having an interest in understanding the process of curriculum adoption and long-term outcomes among the children who had received the curriculum during 2000–2002. In addition, selected teachers who the research staff knew taught lessons the previous year were personally approached to determine their interest.

The planning group also recommended additional team members outside the school where the curriculum was being delivered. These additional members included the district nurse; the health teacher from the middle school where the student assessments would be taking place; and a local curriculum specialist who had experience in student assessment, curriculum development, and teacher professional development. Over the 5-year study period, two of the three original teachers dropped off the committee and were replaced by other teachers recommended and recruited by the project team. In retrospect, it has been noted that we did not have parent representation. Though most team members themselves were parents, and some even had children in the same school district, additional participation by someone explicitly representing parents was an oversight and might have provided a unique perspective and an important voice for INEP in other settings.

Define Stakeholder Roles and Structure for Their Input

The explicit role of project team members was to define the questions to be answered by the evaluation, determine how best to answer those questions, help problem solve implementation issues, and help interpret and disseminate findings. Team members who were not RMPRC staff were expected to contribute by attending a 2-hour meeting eight times per year, a half-day retreat once per year, and additional time meeting or reviewing documents not to exceed a total of 6 hours in any month. Compensation was $750 per year paid in two payments.

RMPRC staff provided technical and administrative support to the team. Community team members took a leadership role for several components of the evaluation, including developing and formatting the lesson feedback form to track curriculum adoption and delivery and reviewing middle school questionnaires used in other studies to identify survey questions that could be used in the student follow-up evaluation. The team curriculum specialist developed the concept and prompt for the CSAP-style writing sample for seventh graders, conducted pilot testing in a nearby community, developed the grading rubric, trained teachers to score the writing samples, and summarized the results.

Each summer, the project team met for a half-day retreat to review the results of data collected in the prior year and to plan for the following year. As part of the retreat, project team members periodically conducted an anonymous self-assessment to evaluate and improve the project team process. Topics on the brief pencil-and-paper survey included whether meetings stayed on task, whether everyone had equal opportunity for input, how comfortable members felt in sharing their thoughts, whether they felt their opinions were considered, whether they were satisfied with the team's progress, whether they felt their skills and expertise were being used, and what they had learned from the process that was valuable to them professionally or personally.

DESCRIBE THE PROGRAM

The long-term goal of INEP is to achieve sustained behavior change in children and secondarily to establish nutrition education as an accepted part of elementary school education. The INEP lessons are built around the following ideas (University of Colorado at Denver and Health Sciences Center, 2007):

- Each lesson has a hands-on component. Experiential learning allows children to explore and interact with their world in a way that helps them better understand it. Food preparation is an effective hands-on strategy to promote healthy eating.
- Some lessons divide the class into small groups. Children learn through cooperation and interaction with each other. Through small group interaction, children can gain skills in communication, sharing, waiting, and taking turns, and they have the opportunity to participate directly in food preparation.
- Each lesson focuses on a specific behavior. Behavior change is the ultimate outcome of health education. The lessons target the following nutrition messages:
  - Eat more fruits and vegetables
  - Eat a balanced diet

- Eat 2 to 3 servings of low-fat dairy products daily
- Eat more whole grains in place of refined grains
- Be more active

• The lessons accomplish academic objectives along with health outcomes, and they are tied to science and literacy standards.

• The lessons are easy to integrate. For example, October includes a healthy bones lesson around Halloween, November includes a lesson about the importance of the family meal around Thanksgiving, December includes holiday celebrations from a variety of cultures, January/February features lessons related to Chinese New Year and Black History Month, and March teaches children how plants grow.

Determine Program Theory or Logic

The intervention design was based on social cognitive theory, Piaget's cognitive development theory, and the educational theories of Dewey. Auld et al. (1998) described the use of theory in INEP as follows:

A classroom intervention was designed that was tied to behavior change theory, considered children's developmental readiness to learn, and was structured to be acceptable to schools and teachers. Tenets of cognitive development theory were translated into classroom activities through the making and eating of food (reliance on senses and experience and the attainment of skills), focusing on how the food tastes now rather than how it affects disease states later (present instead of future focus), emphasizing foods instead of nutrients, de-emphasizing serving sizes, and giving "eat more" messages instead of "moderation" (reliance on concrete instead of abstract or complex concepts). Elementary-aged children's developmental need for concrete experience rather than abstract associations has been noted in research on children's health beliefs as well as the education literature [Contento, 1981; Bush & Iannotti, 1990; Mickalide, 1986].

The experiential aspect of the classroom activities—hands-on food preparation, eating, and working in small groups—is based on education theorists who advocate that knowledge is constructed actively, not received passively—hence the need for children to interact with materials and environment [Bybee & Sund, 1990; Dewey, 1956]. The act of food preparation accomplished this axiom. From a behavior change perspective, studies have been done looking at the associative conditioning from the experience with the food itself and its influence on dietary behavior. Preference has been shown to increase with exposure, tasting (not just smelling or seeing) is essential for acceptance, and positive social affective context is an important influence [Birch, 1987; Birch, Marlin, & Rotter, 1984; Birch, Zimmerman, & Hind, 1980]. The activities were conducted in small groups to allow each child to be actively engaged mentally, emotionally, and physically. Small groups additionally enhanced opportunities for self-discovery and learning from peer interaction. The overall assumption from the experiential aspect of the activities was that being active—making choices, developing strategies, and taking responsibility for one's actions—would facilitate behavior change [Rickard, 1995]. (p. 269)

In planning the evaluation of longer-term outcomes in students, these earlier descriptions of the curriculum were reviewed by the project team. Though we discussed developmental outcomes in the children as potential evaluation outcomes, the team lacked expertise in this area to identify gaps in the literature or appropriate measures (see "Lessons Learned" No. 2).

Another step we took in planning the evaluation was to systematically review all lessons delivered to students during 2000–2002 to better understand how behavioral determinants based in social cognitive theory were incorporated into each of the sessions. The resulting mediational model is illustrated in Figure 3.1 and operationalized in Table 3.1.

FOCUS THE EVALUATION

Over 4 years, the project team developed multiple methods for assessing long-term curriculum effects in students and adoption of the curriculum among teachers. Initially, the project team agreed that student and teacher burden needed to be minimized and that funds to support research staff time in data collection, data management, and analysis were limited. To narrow the scope of the evaluation, the project team addressed a series of questions that helped focus the long-term follow-up component of the evaluation:

- On which components of the dietary behavior do we want to focus?

  What was the focus of the curriculum? The curriculum included lessons designed to address fruit and vegetable intake, fat in foods, and physical activity. Because the majority of the lessons focus on nutrition, it was decided that the evaluation would focus primarily on fruit and vegetable intake.

  Do we want to focus on behaviors that are known to change as children get older? Examples of food behaviors documented to change as children get older included decreased frequency of eating breakfast, decreased consumption of fruits and vegetables, increased consumption of soft drinks, and decreased consumption of milk and fruit juice. The project team agreed that differences in the intervention and comparison cohorts might be easier to detect for behaviors known to change as children grow older.

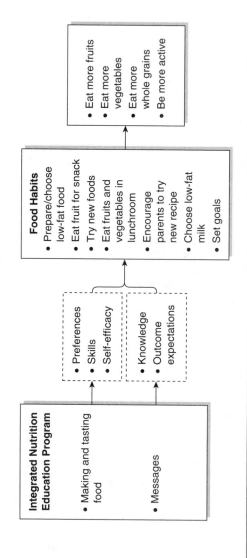

Figure 3.1   Behavioral Determinants Targeted by the Integrated Nutrition Education Program

Table 3.1   Lesson Elements Tied to Theory-Based Behavioral Determinants (2000–2002)

Lesson Elements

Hands-On Experience Making and Tasting Foods

Preferences (through exposure)

- Tasting foods
- Experience with food preparation: reading a recipe; slicing, stirring, and cooking

Skills

- Ability to prepare a recipe: 15 recipes prepared in second grade; 21 recipes prepared in third grade
- Ability to identify foods that contain fat
- Ability to choose foods from different groups on the food pyramid

Self-efficacy

- Confidence in ability to read/prepare a recipe
- Confidence in ability to identify foods with fat
- Confidence in ability to prepare fruits and vegetables
- Confidence in ability to prepare or choose a healthy snack

Health Messages

Knowledge

Food pyramid and 5-a-day

- What foods belong to which groups on the food pyramid?
- How many servings per day should you eat of each food group?

Nutritional properties of food

- What are healthy versus unhealthy ways to eat potatoes?
- Which type of milk has more fat?
- What nutrients does milk contain?
- How can you have strong bones?
- How can you keep your heart healthy?
- How can you identify fat in foods?
- What does fat do for the body?
- Too much fat is bad for your heart and health.
- What kinds of food are low in fat?
- What does protein do for the body?
- Exercise can help keep muscles strong.
- What does vitamin A do for the body?

(Continued)

Table 3.1 (Continued)

- What does calcium do for the body?
- What are the nutritional properties of fruits and vegetables (e.g., which are high in vitamin A)?
- What are the benefits of physical activity?

Attitudes/Outcome Expectations

- Being physically active is fun.
- Cooking/preparing food is fun.
- Fruits and vegetables keep you healthy.
- Physical activity will help you build muscles, strengthen bones, feel better, prevent disease.
- My health is important to me.

Food Habits/Behaviors

- Prepare food with low-fat ingredients.
- Choose fruit for a snack.
- Try new foods.
- Encourage parents to try a lesson recipe.
- Drink low-fat instead of whole milk.
- Ask families to buy low-fat milk.
- Choose snack foods that are low in fat.
- Be physically active with your family.
- Set goals.

- What mediating factors do we want to evaluate?

  What factors did the theoretical bases of the program suggest as mediators? This question was addressed by reviewing early papers published on the curriculum and by talking with the Denver-based project director who had been involved in developing the curriculum.

- What other factors are of interest to us?

  The team considered potential modifying variables that might influence the strength of the relationship between curriculum delivery and long-term outcomes related to knowledge, attitudes, and behavior. This included whether the child perceived that he or she had control over food purchasing and preparation within the home environment, social support, and family-shared activities. In addition, an expanded set of outcome variables was briefly considered (cooperation as a result of working in teams, readiness to learn, school performance). The project team concluded that these were unlikely to be strong enough to be detectable, especially given the length of time that had elapsed since students received the curriculum.

For the curriculum adoption portion of the study, the researchers on the project team determined that there had been limited research regarding how health curricula can best be adapted for sustained use by classroom teachers. The Child and Adolescent Trial for Cardiovascular Health (CATCH) investigators found that six attributes were related to program adoption: relative advantage, compatibility, complexity, trialability, observability, and cost (Hoelscher et al., 2001). Other motivators that were found to increase adoption in CATCH included social praise and school recognition, booster trainings, in-services, and feedback sessions.

The initial set of questions developed by the research team and RMPRC CAB included the following:

- How does use of the curriculum evolve over time, both in terms of overall use and in terms of modifications to the lessons?
- What factors affect adoption and use by teachers?
- What aspects of the curriculum are attractive to teachers?

Once the project team was formed for the evaluation, the group brainstormed about factors that would explain whether teachers continued to use the curriculum (see Figure 3.2). This framework drove the content of the Teacher Feedback Survey filled out by all teachers after delivering each lesson and the qualitative interviews conducted with teachers. The teachers helped design and format the survey so that it was quick and easy to fill out; the response rate has been 98% or higher every year.

Ensure Feasibility

The project team met regularly to discuss the questions we were trying to address with the evaluation, the design, measurement tools, and logistics. Usually the researchers took the lead in gathering existing tools and literature that would be relevant to the discussion and summarizing it in a presentation to the project team. For the purpose of this chapter, we address only feasibility and burden, which may vary depending on the resources available to the evaluation. However, it is also critical to consider the validity and reliability of the information obtained. Table 3.2 presents the measurement methods that the team considered in the planning phase, the perceived feasibility and burden of each, and the final decision about whether the tool was used (and, if it was, in what grades).

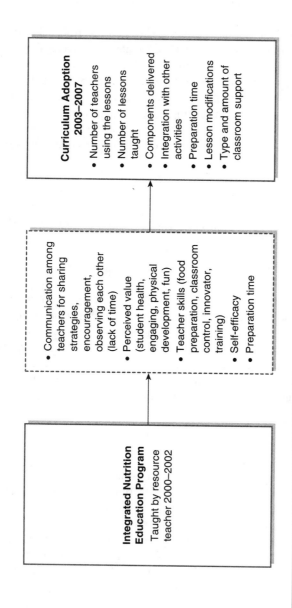

Integrated Nutrition Education Program

Taught by resource teacher 2000–2002

- Communication among teachers for sharing strategies, encouragement, observing each other (lack of time)
- Perceived value (student health, engaging, physical development, fun)
- Teacher skills (food preparation, classroom control, innovator, training)
- Self-efficacy
- Preparation time

Curriculum Adoption 2003–2007

- Number of teachers using the lessons
- Number of lessons taught
- Components delivered
- Integration with other activities
- Preparation time
- Lesson modifications
- Type and amount of classroom support

Figure 3.2   Hypothesized Determinants of Curriculum Adoption

Table 3.2 Assessment of Feasibility and Burden of Possible Evaluation
Methods

Method	Feasibility and Burden	Y/N Grade*
	Long-Term Outcomes in Students	
Height and weight for BMI percentiles	*Feasibility:* High—district nurse interested and willing *Burden:* Moderate—data collection and entry	Y 2–4, 7
24-hour diet recall diet records	*Feasibility:* Low—difficult to schedule individual interviews for each student *Burden:* High—staff time required	N
Plate waste in the lunchroom	*Feasibility:* Low—limited variety of food options available; difficulty discerning which options are healthiest; difficulty reproducing exact lunchroom environment and meal options for intervention and comparison cohorts *Burden:* High—staff time required	N
Food frequency short YRBS form	*Feasibility:* Moderate—teachers were concerned that the abbreviated format would be problematic for sixth graders (i.e., since it is less specific, lots of scenarios would be identified resulting in more questions asked of those administering the survey) *Burden:* Low—only eight questions	N
Food frequency block (long) form	*Feasibility:* Teachers preferred specific food items; easier to administer *Burden:* Moderate—for students and research staff due to greater number of questions	Y 6–8
Survey including food frequency and mediators	*Feasibility:* Moderate—required school approval for class time, sending home passive consents in advance *Burden:* Low—research staff conducted 15-minute training with teachers, teachers used form with prompts provided and read questions to the whole class; required one 45-minute class period; required staff time for data entry and analysis	Y 6, 8

(Continued)

Table 3.2 (Continued)

Method	Feasibility and Burden	Y/N Grade*
Writing sample	*Feasibility:* High—conducted as part of practice writing for standardized testing	Y 7
	Burden: Moderate—pilot testing to refine prompt on 50 students in another district, training of teachers to score; two graders on all writing samples (about 350)	
Student interviews	*Feasibility:* Moderate—requires parent consent and scheduling while the child is on campus	Y 9, 10
	Burden: Moderate—transcription and analysis of interviews	
	Curriculum Adoption by Teachers	
Teacher feedback survey (filled out by teachers after each lesson)	*Feasibility:* High—teachers on the project team were instrumental in developing the questions, wording, and format so that the form was easy to use; return rate has always been over 98%	Y All years
	Burden: Low—for teachers; Moderate—staff time for data entry and analysis	
Teacher interviews	*Feasibility:* High—teachers were willing and available as long as time was scheduled in advance	Y 3 years
	Burden: Moderate—staff and teacher time for interviews, staff time for transcription and analysis	
Team meeting note	*Feasibility:* High—meetings were occurring anyway	Y
	Burden: Low—record and transcribe meeting minutes	

* Yes or no decision by project team on whether to use this method followed by grade level or number of years the assessment was conducted.

LESSONS LEARNED

1. Develop relationships, buy-in, and trust. Probably the single most important factor in a successful evaluation is developing authentic and trusting relationships with people at multiple levels in the organizational structure where the program takes place. This allows for open discussions that help refine the evaluation questions so that they are meaningful and useful. Understanding the decision-making structure and obtaining buy-in among decision makers is important; at the same time, without buy-in from those who are involved in implementation (e.g., teachers), the program may be initiated but not delivered. It may be important to think about connections and relationships outside the school as well. For sustainability, the CAB that originally commissioned the evaluation could have played a bigger role; because of existing relationships, this could have been easily accomplished with increased communication if we had realized CAB's potential role.

2. Consider evaluating factors that influence educational outcomes, and engage collaborators with expertise in child development and education when planning the evaluation. We designed our evaluation to assess student-level outcomes related to the health behaviors addressed in the curriculum. However, as described earlier in this chapter, a central focus of the curriculum developers was to translate cognitive development theory about children's readiness to learn and need for concrete experience and education theory advocating that knowledge is constructed actively, not received passively, into the classroom activities. Teachers recognized that INEP class periods were different from the rest of the children's day. Input from teachers has consistently suggested that INEP teaches cooperation and sharing (social skills that teachers strongly value) and that the students are excited about and look forward to the nutrition lessons. Though this type of feedback has been captured in the evaluation of curriculum adoption, we could have considered additional studies such as assessing student behavior or readiness to learn on days with and without the INEP lessons, or assessing fine motor skill development during the early elementary years comparing students participating in the curriculum with those not participating. Given the current high-stakes environment around academic achievement, we would have increased our chances of demonstrating value to the school district and increased the likelihood of curriculum adoption and sustainability by putting higher priority on behavior, development, and readiness to learn outcomes in the evaluation. Doing so would have required engaging collaborators with expertise in child development and education.

3. Determine if curriculum adaptations have occurred over time and assess whether changes are expected to alter the evaluation findings. In this chapter, we detailed our efforts to understand the curriculum delivered during 2000–2002 in order to inform the long-term effects that were reasonable to expect in children who received the curriculum during that time. Programs change over time for a variety of reasons, and these changes can have positive, negative, or no effects on the outcomes of interest. Examples of changes that occurred in the delivery of INEP included expanding the nutrition emphasis from primarily "eat more fruits and vegetables" to include the more comprehensive dietary guidelines described earlier in this chapter, reducing the number of lessons requiring cooking and heat in the classroom due to one district's fire prevention policies, and adding recent innovations to all lessons to reinforce the health message and encourage children to talk about what they can do to accomplish the recommended health behavior as a summarizing activity at the end of the lesson. In our evaluation, we need to address whether results of long-term follow-up of children who received the curriculum during 2000–2002 would apply to children receiving the curriculum today, or we need to at least describe the curriculum the children were exposed to in sufficient detail and acknowledge that curriculum changes may limit the generalizability of our evaluation results.

4. Understand that with local control comes opportunity and responsibility. The issue of "who has control" is important in planning many evaluations, especially those where the purpose of the evaluation is to determine whether to institute something new on a larger scale or something that requires human or financial resources. Initially, I viewed local control as a by-product of our history in the western frontier and the independence of the early settlers. I now recognize that local control comes with both opportunity and responsibility. Opportunity comes from local knowledge about the community (its needs and how things work) and relationships that can lead to relatively rapid changes compared to changes mandated from a higher level of government. At the same time, there is the responsibility to bring the best information to bear in the local decision-making process. As evaluators, we have the opportunity through thoughtful evaluation planning to provide information that will be useful in the decision-making process at the local level.

5. The sociopolitical environment varies by time and by place. Today, high-stakes testing is a tremendous concern for low-income and low-performing schools. The questions that are important for curriculum adoption vary depending on the current environment. Similarly, the long-term effectiveness of the curriculum is at least partially determined by the availability of healthy choices at school, at home, and in the community, and these factors also vary by place and over time. Recognition is increasing that context can influence the outcome of an intervention or health promotion program; thus, relevant contextual information can inform the generalizability of evaluation findings.

CONCLUSION

Schools are viewed as a convenient setting to reach almost all children in a community for health promotion activities. However, it is critical to recognize and understand the priorities and pressures that play an important role in administrators' and teachers' decisions related to new projects, including school-based program evaluations. At the outset, talk with school administrators so that you have an understanding of the school climate. Develop trusting relationships, be sensitive to time and resource limitations, and find ways to contribute to the school's mission whether or not these activities are directly related to the evaluation. The 90/90/90 observations by Reeves (2000) support curriculum approaches like INEP and evaluation approaches such as the CSAP-style writing sample, which provide a medium for academic learning opportunities and have been found to be common in low-income, high-performing schools. Be open to developmental, behavioral, and academic outcomes in addition to conventional health outcomes, and engage the appropriate stakeholders and experts. These strategies are designed to further the primary mission of our school systems. Finally, understanding and documenting the contextual landscape and adaptations in the curriculum and its delivery over time is important in planning an evaluation that answers meaningful evaluation questions and in helping others interpret and apply the results of your evaluation.

REFERENCES

Auld, G. W., Romaniello, C., Heimendinger, J., Hambidge, C., & Hambidge, M. (1998). Outcomes from a school-based nutrition education program using resource teachers and cross-disciplinary models. *Journal of Nutrition Education, 30,* 268–280.

Auld, G. W., Romaniello, C., Heimendinger, J., Hambidge, C., & Hambidge, M. (1999). Outcomes from a school-based nutrition education program alternating special resource teachers and classroom teachers. *Journal of School Health, 69*(10), 403–408.

Belansky, E. S., Romaniello, C., Morin, C., Uyeki, T., Sawyer, R. L., Scarbro, S., et al. (2006). Adapting and implementing a long-term nutrition and physical activity curriculum to a rural, low-income, biethnic community. *Journal of Nutrition Education and Behavior, 38*(2), 106–113.

Birch, L. L. (1987). The role of experience in children's food acceptance patterns. *Journal of the American Dietetic Association, 87*(9 Suppl.), S36–40.

Birch, L. L., Marlin, D. W., & Rotter, J. (1984). Eating as the "means" activity in a contingency: Effects on young children's food preference. *Child Development, 55,* 431–439.

Birch, L. L., Zimmerman, S. I., & Hind, H. (1980). The influence of social affective context on the formation of children's food preferences. *Child Development, 51*(3), 856–861.

Brett, J. A., Heimendinger, J., Boender, C., Morin, C., & Marshall, J. A. (2002). Using ethnography to improve intervention design. *American Journal of Health Promotion, 16*(6), 331–340.

Bush, P. J., & Iannotti, R. J. (1990). A children's health belief model. *Medical Care, 28*(1), 69–86.

Bybee, R. W., & Sund, R. B. (1990). *Piaget for educators* (2nd ed.). Prospect Heights, IL: Waveland.

Contento, I. R. (1981). Children's thinking about food and eating—A Piagetian-based study. *Journal of Nutrition Education, 13*(1), S86–90.

Dewey, J. (1956). *The child and the curriculum: The school and the society.* Chicago: University of Chicago Press.

Hoelscher, D. M., Kelder, S. H., Murray, N., Cribb, P. W., Conroy, J., Parcel, G. S. (2001). Dissemination and adoption of the child and adolescent trial for cardiovascular health (CATCH): A case study in Texas. *Journal of Public Health Management Practice, 7*(2), 90–100.

Mickalide, A. D. (1986). Children's understanding of health and illness: Implications for health promotion. *Health Values, 10,* 5–21.

Reeves, D. B. (2000). The 90/90/90 schools: A case study. In *Accountability in action: A blueprint for learning organizations* (2nd ed., pp. 185–208). Denver, CO: Advanced Learning.

Rickard, K. (1995). The play approach to learning in the context of families and schools: An alternative paradigm for nutrition and fitness in the 21st century. *Journal of the American Dietetic Association, 95,* 1121–1126.

Sanders, W. L., Saxton, A. M., & Horn, S. P. (1997). The Tennessee value-added assessment system: A quantitative, outcomes-based approach to educational measurement. In J. Millman (Ed.), *Grading teachers, grading schools. Is student achievement a valid evaluation measure?* (pp. 137–162). Thousand Oaks, CA: Corwin.

Stone, J. E. (1999). Value-added assessment: An accountability revolution. In M. Kanstoroom & C. E. Finn, Jr. (Eds.), *Better teachers, better schools* (pp. 239–249). Washington, DC: Thomas B. Fordham Foundation.

University of Colorado at Denver and Health Sciences Center, Department of Pediatrics, Section of Nutrition. (2007). *The integrated nutrition education program lesson book 2007–2008: Focus on science and literacy 2nd grade.* (Available from University of Colorado at Denver and Health Sciences Center, C225-INEP, 4200 E. 9th Ave, Denver, CO 80262).

Vollmer and Associates. (2001). *Schools cannot do this alone.* Retrieved from http://www.jamievollmer.com/burden.doc

4

PLANNING FOR A SERVICE PROGRAM EVALUATION

Mari Millery

Service program is a broad concept, encompassing a large proportion of the settings where evaluations occur. The focus here is on evaluation studies conducted within a single social, health, or human services organization. Each service organization presents a unique context for evaluation planning. This chapter describes an evaluation study planned and implemented at the Leukemia & Lymphoma Society (LLS), highlighting issues of particular importance in service program evaluation planning.

BACKGROUND ON SERVICE PROGRAM CASE STUDY: THE LEUKEMIA & LYMPHOMA SOCIETY PATIENT NAVIGATION EVALUATION

The planning process for this evaluation project started with an e-mail from a colleague who had been contacted by LLS for help recruiting an evaluator. LLS wanted an evaluation of its Information Resource Center (IRC) and specifically of the enhanced patient navigation service it was planning to implement at IRC. Based on the match between the program and my academic interests and expertise, I was eager to pursue this opportunity and successfully responded to the request for proposals (RFP). Our planning dialogue began with some initial conversations about questions I raised while writing the proposal. Though the RFP and proposal were helpful starting points for our initial conversations, the details of the study emerged throughout the ensuing planning process.

LLS describes itself as the "world's largest voluntary health organization dedicated to funding blood cancer research, education, and patient services" (LLS, 2004). A private nonprofit service organization funded by individual and corporate contributions, LLS has 68 chapters across the United States and Canada. The LLS IRC, staffed with trained, master's-prepared information specialists, responds to nearly 80,000 inquiries a year from leukemia, lymphoma, myeloma, and other blood cancer patients, patients' family members, and health care professionals. IRC services, which include providing information, guidance, and support to callers, are mostly delivered via telephone.

According to the RFP, IRC wanted to "pilot a patient navigation model to continue to service patients that come to [IRC] with scheduled follow-up services." Patient navigation generally refers to helping patients navigate the health care system and overcome barriers to care (Dohan & Schrag, 2005; Fowler, Steakley, Garcia, Kwok, & Bennett, 2006; Freeman, 2006). Essentially, the plan was to conduct a pilot evaluation of a service enhancement consisting of scheduled follow-up telephone calls by information specialists to selected callers. The need for the enhancement was identified by program staff, who felt that many callers could benefit from extended contact with IRC.

Like many service organizations, LLS is passionate about serving its client population. Because most service organizations are busy with service delivery and often do not have access to extensive evaluation resources, they may place evaluation low among competing priorities. However, this is not true for LLS, which values evaluation and has instituted that view in the organizational culture. This commitment to evaluation was evidenced in initial conversations by statements like, "We evaluate all new programs before full launch and evaluate existing programs on an ongoing basis, making changes as needed based on evaluation data," and supported by the relative ease of engaging program staff throughout the project. The funding for the evaluation described here came from within LLS.

The initial planning for the pilot evaluation—from the date of the initial e-mail from my colleague to the launch of the pilot program—unfolded over 3 months. Six months later, I submitted the final report for the pilot study. Encouraged by the results of the pilot study, LLS decided to sponsor a second, larger evaluation of patient navigation, which required another several months of planning. The description that follows, using the Evaluation Planning Incorporating Context (EPIC) model, is primarily about the initial planning steps taken before the pilot study.

ASSESS CONTEXT

Trying to understand a service program without knowing the context is like reading one sentence in this book without the rest of the text. The "text" around service programs often includes complex organizational hierarchies and affiliations, the origins of the program funding and design, the specific characteristics of the population receiving the services, and other programs offering similar or related services. A variety of models exist for the relationship between the service program, the evaluation sponsor, and the evaluator, including external and internal evaluators and external and internal evaluation funding. Each of these models places the evaluator in a different position within the context.

Understand the Political and Organizational Environment

Before this evaluation project, I knew very little about LLS. To plan the evaluation study, I quickly had to learn as much as possible about this organization. I consulted a variety of information sources, including people inside and outside LLS, the Internet, LLS promotional materials, and the RFP for the evaluation study. Many service organizations have a mission statement, which can be a great starting point. An organization's Web site and other promotional materials can also be extremely informative. It was helpful to gain some early understanding of the size and scope of the organization, its key activities, and its organizational structure. A list of questions generated during the initial planning stages served as a helpful tool throughout the evaluation planning process (see Table 4.1).

Working with service organizations can be inspiring because of their passion for helping their clients. This spirit of commitment to the cause defines the organizational culture of agencies such as LLS. Though this was not the case with our study, the emphasis on client service can sometimes have a negative influence on evaluation. For example, the evaluation may be viewed as taking resources away from direct services. The commitment to the client population is often connected to a broader context of advocacy. For instance, LLS has an advocacy program that "promotes increased federal funding of biomedical research and influences healthcare reform issues, including ready access to quality cancer care and insurance coverage or patient-care costs in clinical trials" (LLS, 2005). It is important to understand the politics surrounding relevant advocacy issues, and an evaluator who is new to the issues can get some initial grounding simply by searching the Internet or other news media for recent information.

Table 4.1   Examples of Questions Evaluator Noted During Early Planning

Question	Comments on How to Ask the Question
Where is the money coming from for the evaluation study?	Ask early on.
Why are they posing some of these very specific questions (e.g., wanting to target callers from Wyoming)?	Let them explain their intentions first, and then ask this as a clarifying question.
Where does the patient navigation model come from?	Do background research first, and then bring up in the first meeting.
How did they arrive at the study design specifications listed in the RFP (e.g., callers surveyed at baseline and at 1 and 2 months after initial call)?	Save for later discussion; not necessary in first meeting.
How long is the average call handled by the IRC?	Weave question into initial conversations.
Should we do process evaluation?	Ask after some discussion of their outcome evaluation plans.

One significant characteristic of LLS as a service organization is its funding, which consists of individual and corporate contributions. LLS's management model differs somewhat from what I had seen in service programs sponsored by federal or local government agencies, even those that were part of nonprofit or community-based organizations. LLS operates more like a private sector organization and indicated a high level of concern for accountability to donors. This management model has implications for how evaluation findings are used and for how funding decisions are made regarding programs and program evaluation.

Getting a sense of the organizational infrastructure of the agency is a central task in the initial assessment of the program context. Service programs can operate on many organizational levels and are often embedded in complex organizational structures. The evaluator needs to identify the location of the particular service program in various departmental and reporting structures. The administrative structures of LLS emerged from reading the background materials and became more concrete once I visited the organization. It was important to see how IRC is structured as a department within LLS and that IRC has to make a case to the LLS national board of trustees to obtain funding for a program such as patient navigation. In a sense, the patient navigation program competes for funding within the organization, and program evaluation findings become an important way to make the case for program funding.

As noted earlier, LLS values program evaluation and uses evaluation findings to inform funding decisions. Knowing this helped me understand the motivation behind the evaluation study, which was essentially to obtain objective data on a program enhancement under consideration for routine implementation. We could then plan the evaluation design and timeline to accommodate this decision-making context. In this case, we wanted a simple study designed to test the effectiveness of the program enhancement within our timeline.

IRC was the immediate organizational program context in which the pilot enhancement program was to be implemented and evaluated. Based on the RFP, the other background materials I had gathered, and my conversations with LLS representatives, I developed an increasingly clear understanding of how IRC operates and how patient navigation fits into it. It was essential to gauge the size and scope of the program early on: IRC has seven full-time information specialists who answer nearly 80,000 phone calls a year. The center plans to offer patient navigation to a subgroup of callers and perhaps dedicate two information specialists to this program. This picture emerged only gradually over the first few months.

To fully appreciate the logistics of the operation, I had to see IRC in action. It is much easier to start planning for a study when the evaluator has a clear picture of how the service is provided. For example, once I saw IRC's operation, it was easier for me to imagine ways for information specialists to introduce the evaluation study and the survey to potential study participants; I also could suggest specific ideas for handling the logistics of survey mailings.

Because the patient navigation enhancement was a new activity, it was appropriate for LLS to commission a pilot study. The RFP outlined the idea of patient navigation and the expected outcomes of interest, which gave the evaluation project a great head start. One of my first tasks was to interpret the RFP and to flesh out the context around it. For example, the RFP did not explain where the concept of patient navigation originated or whether there was a theoretical or conceptual framework behind it. I raised these questions in our early conversations as part of my efforts to assess the context. As noted previously, my running list of clarifications and follow-up questions was helpful during the early stages and enabled me to ask the right questions at the right time. However, in the initial meetings, it is not appropriate to bombard stakeholders with a long list of questions, some of which may be sensitive in nature.

It was also essential for me to understand that LLS is a national organization that operates a network of 68 local chapters that implement local-level activities. This was important because a key objective of IRC, which serves the entire United States, is to link callers to their local chapters. This linkage was one of the key outcomes IRC hoped to improve through patient navigation.

Outside of LLS is a complex landscape of cancer information services. Though I did not learn much about this aspect of the context during the early planning stages, in retrospect, viewing LLS within this context early on could have been helpful. The need for consumer-friendly cancer information is enormous (Rutten, Squiers, & Hesse, 2006). While many organizations, including LLS, specialize in disseminating information on particular types of cancer, the National Cancer Institute (NCI) of the National Institutes of Health operates a well-documented and well-researched information service covering all types of cancer (Darrow, Speyer, Marcus, Ter Maat, & Krome, 1998; Freimuth, Stein, & Kean, 1989; Muha, Smith, Baum, Ter Maat, & Ward, 1998; Ward, Baum, Ter Maat, Thomsen, & Maibach, 1998). Other countries have large cancer information services as well, such as the British Association of Cancer United Patients (Venn et al., 1996). NCI and the other organizations frequently collaborate, constituting a community of cancer information service professionals. For evaluation planning, it would have been useful to study reports produced by these organizations on their information services. This type of research would have confirmed early on that the patient navigation model was an innovative approach to providing cancer information services.

Define the Relationship Between the Evaluator and the Sponsor

Service program evaluations are conducted through a variety of staffing and funding arrangements (e.g., internal or external evaluator, internal or external funding). Many organizations have internal evaluation staff who use a combination of internal and external funding for their work. Sometimes a proposal is written for external funding, and an external evaluation partner gets involved during proposal development. This evaluation study did not have a third-party funding agency as a sponsor. In this case, the funding for the evaluation came from within LLS, but I was hired as an external evaluator. The role of the LLS national board of trustees in approving the LLS yearly budget was somewhat analogous to that of a sponsor in that the findings were to be reported to the board. However, the LLS Vice President for Patient Services and Disease Programs, which includes IRC, served as the point of contact with me throughout the project in terms of evaluation funding and reporting of results.

Each type of evaluator–sponsor relationship has advantages and disadvantages. For example, internal evaluators can work more seamlessly as part of the program, but they may be more susceptible to internal pressure to obtain positive findings. In contrast, external evaluators can lend objectivity and credibility to the evaluation study, but they often spend significant time learning about the program and building relationships with stakeholders. Sometimes external funding is targeted for only an evaluation study, but more typically it funds both a specific program and its evaluation. The evaluator should be aware of the potential biases introduced by the various evaluator-sponsors, and evaluation funding arrangements and should clarify roles and relationships early in the planning process. The evaluator may also have to educate the sponsor and other stakeholders about the advantages and disadvantages of a particular funding arrangement.

In this case, LLS and I established a participatory relationship for planning and implementing the study, in which we made all important decisions together as we planned and designed the study. This relationship was implemented through an initial meeting in person, frequent subsequent contact by phone and e-mail, and another in-person meeting later in the planning process. LLS was represented by two managers, one IRC supervisor, and one IRC staff member. One of the managers and the supervisor served as the ongoing liaisons with me.

LLS staff continuously educated me about their program, and I educated them about feasible study design options. I had primary responsibility for drafting study-related documents, but LLS staff provided frequent feedback. In order for the participatory process to work, it was important for me to accurately assess the stakeholders' level of knowledge about evaluation and research design and then involve and educate them appropriately. I was fortunate to have a group of partners who knew something about research design, as one of their roles is to translate cancer research studies into patient education. However, even this audience required education about issues such as control groups (e.g., verifying their importance) and sample sizes (e.g., explaining how adequate sample sizes are determined).

The evaluator's background and how it matches the sponsor's needs is also important. Ideally, the evaluator will have relevant previous experience in the specific domain of the study. In this case, I was attracted to the evaluation opportunity specifically because it was a good fit with my overall professional interest in health information seeking. I had other projects under way that examined issues in consumers' use of health information, and I was familiar with literature in this area. Establishing whether the evaluator has the expertise for a certain type of research is one reason for quickly gathering initial background information and making some preliminary assessments. For example, evaluators vary in their capacity to conduct quantitative and qualitative analyses; even with my relatively strong background in quantitative survey research, I needed to seek out statistical expertise to validate my power analysis (assessment of the required sample size).

Determine the Level of the Evaluation

My study with LLS is an example of an evaluation that was essentially local in nature even though the scope of the program is nationwide. The program is both local and national because the community of cancer patients is not geographically defined but rather is dependent on a distance-based service modality (i.e., telephone). Furthermore, a key goal of IRC is to connect clients to their local LLS chapters.

In the RFP, LLS had designated particular categories of clients to target for patient navigation: newly diagnosed patients, patients seeking information on clinical trials, and patients residing in Wyoming. LLS staff clarified that the target categories for the intervention had been selected after carefully considering where patient navigation could help the most. Specific target groups were identified for two reasons: (1) because resources were too limited to offer the intervention to all callers and (2) because the patient navigation approach emphasizes reduction of health disparities for patient groups that are particularly vulnerable (Fowler et al., 2006). When discussing the target groups, LLS staff explained that Wyoming was targeted because there was no active LLS local chapter in that state and LLS hoped the navigation service would fill that gap. Though questions remained about obtaining a sufficient sample size to separately evaluate calls received from Wyoming, we decided to proceed with the original set of target groups.

Determining the level of evaluation is parallel to clarifying the purpose of the evaluation. In this case, clarification was needed on such issues as whether the study should be restricted to patient navigation and how much to focus on outcomes versus process. During our discussions, it was helpful to articulate different iterations of the study purpose in writing. The RFP indicated that LLS was primarily interested in obtaining outcomes. We decided that we should also include a process component because this was a new program enhancement, and we wanted to explore and document how it was done; however, the primary purpose of the study remained at the outcomes level. This discussion consumed a significant portion of our initial meeting.

Service program evaluations often include a process-level component. Where there is a service, there is a service delivery process, and that process needs to be documented and understood even when the ultimate interest is to show that the service has an impact on an outcome. Measurement of "outputs" (e.g., number of clients served) is often central to service program evaluations. Many service programs have also instituted quality assurance or continuous quality improvement programs that intersect, and sometimes overlap, with program evaluation efforts in general and process evaluation efforts in particular (McLaughlin & Kaluzny, 1999). Later in the planning process (during a conversation about survey question wording), I learned that IRC had conducted an evaluation survey with callers a few years before that focused on client satisfaction with IRC services. My discovery of the previous survey led me to request more information about it. Establishing the level of evaluation in a service program is also about situating the evaluation study within related efforts, such as quality improvement projects and other evaluation studies.

GATHER RECONNAISSANCE

The reconnaissance step of the EPIC model involves finding out more about how the evaluation findings will be used and validating commitment to the evaluation. Both of these topics are important to address in the context of service programs.

Specify Evaluation Uses

The RFP did not fully explain why an evaluation of the patient navigation program was needed. It stated that "the pilot study will determine if the IRC will revise its service model moving forward to offer patient navigation services." Understanding the evaluation uses required interpretation of the RFP and conversations with LLS contacts. Focusing on articulating the purpose of the evaluation was key because it revealed information about planned uses for findings and various motivations for the evaluation. This information can help in planning the best possible study but cannot necessarily be ascertained through direct questioning of stakeholders. If the evaluator asks the wrong question at the wrong time or addresses a question to the wrong person, he or she can be perceived as arrogant, ignorant, or impatient. Thus, it is important to keep a record of questions as they emerge so they can be addressed at the right time through the appropriate channels.

At one point during the pilot study, when deadlines for evaluation reports were discussed, it became clear that the findings would be used to make decisions about continuing the patient navigation program and that the amount of funding to IRC was at stake. LLS is an evaluation-friendly organization, but that also means that evaluations are used to make decisions and thus become part of the organization's internal programmatic and funding politics.

Nobody likes to get negative results in evaluation studies. Service programs in particular want to show positive outcomes that demonstrate program impact on clients. However, it is useful for the evaluator to consider the consequences of "negative" results early in the planning process. What would the consequences be if the study results do not show program impact? The answer to that question can reveal a lot about the intended uses of the evaluation.

Questions about the evaluation uses can be part of the evaluator's running list of questions. These may be among the questions to be listed because the evaluator cannot directly pose them to stakeholders right away. The hope is that answers will emerge during the process, including clarification on the uses of the evaluation. The goal of the planning process is to articulate the purpose of the evaluation as clearly as possible in the evaluation plan. Once the uses of the evaluation are better understood, the purpose of the study can be more accurately stated. In this case, the purpose of the evaluation could not be articulated until the planning process was complete. The RFP written by LLS and the subsequent proposal written by me were very helpful, but, in retrospect, some aspects of the study were prematurely defined in those documents. For example, it was too early to specify time intervals for follow-up surveys. These early documents also overemphasized outcomes over the process. The actual details were worked out over several months. This illustrates that the evaluation study design cannot be determined without a proper planning process.

Another use of the evaluation findings that we discussed only briefly during the planning stage was to disseminate the findings beyond this particular organization and examine the results in the context of relevant literature. It is useful to articulate this type of use early in the process and even to have preliminary discussions about plans for potential publications and other dissemination activities. Doing so orients everyone to a commonly agreed-on direction and sets the stage for later negotiations about dissemination matters such as coauthorship.

Validate Perspectives

All of my initial contact with LLS was through two individuals from LLS management who were very enthusiastic about the evaluation project. The support and cooperation of the IRC staff was subsequently validated when I met with them. An IRC supervisor became involved in the planning after the initial stage, and I personally met all IRC staff members face-to-face during my visit to the call center. Problems with staff buy-in are not uncommon in service program evaluation. When I met IRC staff and had a chance to conduct a very brief informal interview with each of them, I looked for signs of resistance to the evaluation, but I did not detect any. All questions they raised were in the spirit of facilitating the implementation of the study, and they appeared to be genuinely interested in working with me on this project.

The evaluator needs to imagine what an evaluation means from the stakeholders' perspectives, particularly the frontline service staff and their supervisors. This kind of exercise quickly reveals that evaluation can be seen as intrusive and threatening. This is equally important in a seemingly evaluation-friendly setting such as LLS, where resistance to evaluation may be more subtle. It is important to state clearly that the evaluation is about the program, not about the staff, and to acknowledge that the evaluation activities may introduce an additional burden on the staff. An ongoing assessment of the organization's commitment to the evaluation is particularly important in service organizations, especially when they do not have a proevaluation culture like LLS. High turnover among staff and management in the service sector is another reason for ongoing assessment of commitment.

ENGAGE STAKEHOLDERS

Potential stakeholders for a service program include, at a minimum, program management, program staff, program clients, and the sponsor. In this case, the stakeholders involved in the evaluation planning consisted of program management and staff. I did not have an opportunity to obtain direct input from clients or the sponsor (i.e., LLS national board of trustees).

There are two main reasons why the evaluator must engage stakeholders in evaluation planning. First, stakeholders possess a unique level of understanding of the program. Therefore, they can help ensure the validity of the evaluation study (i.e., confirm that the study corresponds with the real nature of the program). Second, the evaluator needs stakeholders' cooperation to conduct the study. Data collection frequently burdens staff and clients in significant ways. Engaging stakeholders as partners helps secure their buy-in and lessens the sense of threat stakeholders sometimes associate with evaluation. For these reasons, it is particularly important that service program evaluations engage program staff and, if possible, program clients as well.

Identify and Invite Stakeholders

Even evaluators with the best technical research expertise cannot be successful if they fail to build rapport with stakeholders. The best way to establish rapport is to show respect for stakeholders' expertise. In our case, the stakeholders involved in the evaluation planning were a group of key management and staff members (two LLS managers, one IRC supervisor, and one IRC staff member). I conducted the planning of the study in close partnership with this group of stakeholders. Other stakeholders were identified but not actively involved in study planning. In retrospect, the client perspective could have been useful in the early stages. When the service organization has a client advisory board or similar mechanism in place, this may become an avenue for engaging clients in evaluation planning. We did not have such a structure available, and it was not possible to pursue client input given the brief time frame in which to complete the study. Later, when surveys started coming in from participants, we realized that some respondents were eager to offer us advice and feedback, especially on the format of the survey questions, which demonstrated that they were in fact an important voice to be heard. For example, many of them wanted to elaborate on reasons why they did not accomplish particular actions following their interaction with IRC, and, in retrospect, our survey questions should have probed these explanations.

LLS's national board of trustees, which in this internally funded study served in a "sponsor" role, can be considered an important stakeholder. The board, which governs all LLS activities, is a diverse group of more than 30 members across the United States, including professionals serving cancer patients, medical experts, family members of cancer patients, and business and legal professionals. They were the ultimate audience for the evaluation results, but I did not have direct contact with the board during the planning process; the two representatives of LLS management who worked with me handled all communication with the board.

Define Stakeholder Roles and Structure for Their Input

This evaluation study did not attempt to engage a complex set of multiple stakeholder groups, mainly because of the restricted timeline for planning the study. However, the importance of engaging the few stakeholder groups that were involved in study planning and implementation should not be underestimated. These groups included LLS management, IRC supervisors, IRC information specialists, and IRC clerical staff. The roles of these groups vis-à-vis the evaluation project were defined in the evaluation plan. Before the evaluation plan was finalized, the roles were delineated in the work plan that was part of my original evaluation proposal. The principle underlying the roles was the participatory relationship between the evaluator and the LLS stakeholders. For example, it was explicitly stated that the study design and the survey instruments would be collaboratively designed. This meant that part of the role definition for two LLS managers, one IRC supervisor, and one IRC information specialist involved participating in the study design and instrument design processes. This arrangement worked well because it allowed the staff expertise to directly inform decisions such as the wording of survey questions. It is important to find a mechanism for this kind of program-level input, even in cases where staff have limited expertise with evaluation issues, such as survey design.

Establish Group Processes for Ongoing Stakeholder Involvement

The proposal work plan, and subsequently the evaluation plan, included a process for involving the key stakeholders. Our plan referred to ongoing communication, though we did not specify meeting or communication frequency or modality. Some of the communication process was planned outside of the formal documentation. For example, an IRC supervisor was assigned to be the primary liaison to communicate with me once the study was launched. Having one ongoing contact person at the program level turned out to be very helpful. The communication processes for stakeholder involvement were ongoing and multimodal during the planning and implementation stages of the study. We used telephone, e-mail, and in-person meetings both at my office and at the program site. All study-related documentation circulated back and forth for comments. I made sure every comment from LLS was considered and acknowledged; those I could not incorporate were discussed.

In the evaluation plan timeline, we specified due dates for preliminary and final evaluation reports. Many of these report deadlines were based on when program funding decisions would need to be made. The preliminary reports were critically important in terms of providing opportunities for ongoing stakeholder input. Even the pilot study, which took 9 months to complete, included a plan for both a preliminary and a final evaluation report. We followed that plan and found the preliminary report to be extremely informative. Discussions about the preliminary report improved stakeholder involvement by enabling them to see concretely what they could learn from the evaluation data.

DESCRIBE THE PROGRAM

Once the evaluator has a sufficient understanding of the context and stakeholder involvement has been established, the next step is for the evaluator to become immersed in the nature of the program to be evaluated. At this point, we had determined that this was a pilot evaluation study for a new program enhancement that would be implemented within a well-established service program. The IRC service, which consists of answering telephone inquiries from cancer patients and their family members, was to be enhanced with a patient navigation intervention consisting of IRC staff making follow-up calls to clients to provide additional information, guidance, and support. We also had some notion of where the program originated and what the conceptual framework was. The basic idea for the program appeared to be relatively simple. However, this seemingly simple program enhancement raised a lot of questions: Which patients will be called back? By whom and at what point? What will be discussed on the follow-up calls? What outcomes are expected to be improved by these follow-up calls?

The Centers for Disease Control and Prevention (CDC) "Framework for Program Evaluation in Public Health" defines several key aspects to be covered in a program description (CDC, 1999). For example, it is helpful to formulate a statement of need that describes the problem or opportunity that the program addresses. In this case, a need for the program enhancement had been identified, though not formally documented, by the program staff. It had become clear that one phone conversation was not sufficient to provide callers the level of IRC service that many of them need and that a follow-up conversation would be an opportunity to deliver a better service. CDC also highlights the importance of identifying the expected effects of the program. This is where evaluators need to probe stakeholders to find out how they define success. A significant amount of time was spent with the

LLS stakeholders discussing what they saw as the potential benefits of the follow-up calls and what changes they expected in patients as a result of the follow-up calls.

I cannot emphasize enough the importance of observing the program in person. I was fortunate to be able to visit IRC, speak with the staff, and hear them describe how they work. By doing this, the numbers I had about the volume of the operation were given a real meaning in terms of staff activities. Even though I had been given access to very good written documentation about the program, I needed the visit to fully understand and describe it. To imagine the flow of the service process, it was useful to see how the cubicles in the space were organized, surrounded by a wealth of resource materials, and how the information specialists, who sat in their cubicles using a headphone and a microphone while typing on the computer, organized their workspaces to maximize efficient workflow.

Conceptualize Program Theory or Rationale

Logic models and conceptual models are very useful at this stage of the planning process to help clarify different levels of outcomes and relate those outcomes to activities and outputs. Service programs often have an ultimate aim of improving clients' lives, for example, in terms of life expectancy, clinical health outcomes, or quality of life. However, the appropriate term of outcome for the evaluation study may be more intermediate, such as behavior change or increased knowledge, which in turn is expected to lead to the ultimate outcomes. Because we saw this as a relatively straightforward study, we did not use a formal logic model or conceptual model during the planning process. However, we sketched out several diagrams and chains of outcomes to clarify these issues.

Table 4.2 shows an evaluation planning matrix (EPM) that was constructed for this study after the fact. It lists the evaluation questions we considered, classifies them as either process or outcome questions, and groups them by domain of interest. The EPM also lists whether each question is about short-term, intermediate, or long-term outcomes and identifies relevant data sources corresponding to each question. This is the sort of EPM we would have constructed had we decided to use one, but our planning process was quick, and the study was relatively small and simple, so we did not apply formal planning tools. However, if I were to do it again, I would try to construct an EPM. I believe it would have been particularly helpful in keeping track of the potential evaluation questions to be prioritized, and it probably would have made the process more efficient.

Table 4.2 Evaluation Planning Matrix for LLS Patient Navigation

Type of Question	Domain of Interest	Evaluation Question	Term of Outcome	Data Source
Process	Process of patient navigation	What occurs during the patient navigation intervention?	Short	LLS computer system, IRC staff
		What services do callers receive during the navigation follow-up calls?	Short	LLS computer system, caller surveys
	Implementation of patient navigation	What challenges are encountered in implementing patient navigation?	Short	IRC staff
		What is the staffing structure needed for patient navigation?	Short	LLS computer system, IRC staff
		What are the IRC logistics needed for patient navigation?	Short	IRC staff
	Navigation recipients	Who received the patient navigation (types of patients)?	Short	LLS computer system, caller surveys
		Do the callers like the patient navigation?	Short	Caller surveys
		Can most callers be reached for follow-up calls, and are they receptive to the calls?	Short	LLS computer system, IRC staff
Outcome	Utilization of IRC recommendations	Do callers follow up on IRC recommendations? If so, which recommendations?	Intermediate	Caller surveys

Type of Question	Domain of Interest	Evaluation Question	Term of Outcome	Data Source
Outcome (continued)	Ability to link with resources and services	Does the patient navigation help link patients to resources, services, and opportunities? If so, which ones?	Intermediate	Caller surveys
		Are navigation patients more likely to access resources through their local LLS chapter?	Intermediate	Caller surveys
		Does the patient navigation help remove barriers to access to the latest treatment options or services? If so, what barriers?	Intermediate	Caller surveys
		Does the patient navigation enhance continuity of care and services?	Long	Caller surveys
	Success in navigating resources	Do navigation patients perceive success in navigating resources?	Intermediate	Caller surveys
		Do navigation patients have improved knowledge and comprehension of information provided by IRC?	Intermediate	Caller surveys
	Confidence in discussing disease with others	Are navigation patients more confident in discussing treatment with the health care team?	Intermediate	Caller surveys
		Are navigation patients more confident in discussing disease with their family or social network?	Intermediate	Caller surveys
	Enhanced coping	Does the patient navigation enhance coping?	Intermediate	Caller surveys
		Does the patient navigation provide helpful additional emotional support?	Intermediate	Caller surveys
		Does the patient navigation help improve patients' quality of life?	Long	Caller surveys
	Variations in outcomes	Do the outcomes vary by type of patient?		Caller surveys

Many of the evaluation questions listed in the EPM were in the original RFP crafted by LLS or in the proposal I wrote in response to the RFP. Additional evaluation questions emerged during the planning process. The EPM reflects our decision to focus on outcome evaluation while also including a process evaluation component. The process questions explore the nature of the intervention, what it takes to implement it, and the characteristics and perceptions of the participants. The outcome questions were based on what the LLS team and I determined to be the best indicators of success for patient navigation and what we envisioned as possible to obtain through follow-up surveys. At that point, we were considering follow-up telephone or mail surveys with participants and had preliminarily agreed that a control or comparison group was probably feasible; thus, we referred to a survey in the data source column and asked questions that implied a comparison group (e.g., "Are navigation patients more likely to access resources through their local LLS chapter?"). Most of the outcome questions were phrased in terms of intermediate outcomes. They focused on utilization of IRC recommendations, ability to link with resources and services, success in navigating resources, confidence discussing disease with others, and coping. Questions about program impact on continuity of care and quality of life, which represent more extended outcomes, were also considered.

FOCUS THE EVALUATION

Focusing the evaluation involves clarifying the study objectives and finalizing the list of evaluation questions. The planning process should result in a written evaluation plan that articulates as clearly as possible the study objectives, questions, design, and timeline. Our study design team, consisting of the evaluator, two LLS managers, one LLS supervisor, and one LLS staff member, had narrowed the study to a process and outcome evaluation of the patient navigation program enhancement. We composed a list of preliminary evaluation questions, which we continued to focus. We knew that we probably could not address all questions on our list, one obvious limitation being the length of the survey to be given to participants. We began prioritizing our evaluation questions while simultaneously starting a more serious dialogue about study design options. This was accomplished in further phone conferences and document exchanges, as well as an additional in-person meeting of the group. The LLS managers and I mutually guided the process, but more evaluator guidance would probably have been necessary in a less evaluation-savvy context.

At this stage, theoretical frameworks can be used to conceptually organize the outcomes and indicators of interest. In our case, the evaluation questions had largely emerged without tying them to any particular conceptual framework, although some of the terms we used (such as *coping, barriers, continuity of care,* and *quality of life*) were associated with particular conceptual models. I proposed framing some of our outcomes in terms of self-efficacy, which is a concept widely applied in public health programs (Bandura, 1997) and which appeared to fit well with our model of patient navigation. When I briefly described the concept of self-efficacy, which some of the LLS representatives recognized, and explained the benefit of having a conceptual model, the LLS partners immediately liked the idea.

Ensure Feasibility

The discussions where we prioritized the evaluation questions and considered different study designs were essentially about feasibility. We had constraints in terms of resources—the scope of the evaluation budget—and a particularly tight timeline of 6 months in which to complete the pilot study. We agreed that process and outcome questions should be included and that there were relatively straightforward key outcomes that were a priority, such as whether callers follow up on IRC recommendations. Some of the more elusive longer-term outcomes, such as quality of life and continuity of care, were not feasible to address in the study given the limited study timeline; it also was probably a good idea to first establish the program's impact on more immediate outcomes.

The question of a control or comparison group was very important. Knowing that randomized studies are frequently not feasible in service program evaluations, I recognized how fortunate I was to be working with an organization that had written an RFP that outlined a plan to have a comparison group. Because calls coming in to IRC are randomly assigned to information specialists, we could designate two information specialists to the patient navigation program to implement the intervention arm of the study, with a comparison group consisting of comparable clients who were served by other information specialists. Thus, although a true randomized controlled trial was not feasible, we could achieve a good balance of study design rigor and program practicalities.

Assess Potential Data Collection Burden

The data collection burden was an issue on two levels: how much surveying could the participants tolerate and what kinds of data collection operation could IRC take on. The length of the survey had become an issue even before a single survey item was designed. Fortunately, we had prioritized the evaluation questions, because even with the shorter list of questions our initial drafts of the survey were too long. We also had to calculate IRC's capacity to conduct the data collection, especially once we decided that respondents would receive reminder surveys in addition to the initial survey mailing. Other kinds of data that we planned to use for the process evaluation were part of the LLS computer system that IRC routinely uses. We had to discuss the process and burden involved in obtaining those data from the system. For example, LLS staff explained to me what it entails to submit a data request and obtain files from the LLS information technology department and that this was not always easy to accomplish. We then had to decide how much we wanted to rely on the LLS computer system data.

Sample size is a question related to data collection burden. The evaluator's expertise in research design is needed here to inform the discussions in terms of the sample size needed to draw conclusions from the results. Basic procedures of power analysis and an ability to quickly offer rough estimates of required sample sizes come in handy at this stage of planning. This enabled me to insist on a sufficiently large sample. The LLS partners did not have any sense of the required sample size, and they relied on my expertise. For the bigger study conducted after the pilot study, we consulted with a biostatistician to ensure that our power analysis was on target.

LESSONS LEARNED

Each service program is unique and has a unique context and set of stakeholders. Service programs also have varying models of evaluator/sponsor/program relationships, and, like LLS, they often connect to an advocacy context as well as a context of other programs offering similar services. It is helpful to start with the organization's mission statement, if one is available, and to gauge the size and scope of activities of the organization and the program. It is important to understand the organization's attitudes regarding evaluation, as well as the stakeholders' level of knowledge about evaluation and research design. The LLS case study illustrates an environment where the orientation toward evaluation was positive and stakeholders were somewhat knowledgeable about research. It is also helpful to fully understand what is at stake with an evaluation study in terms of potential programmatic decisions, funding, and other consequences.

The evaluator must utilize the stakeholders' expertise about the program. This ensures the validity of the study and minimizes resistance to the evaluation. As our example illustrates, stakeholders can inform the formulation of a statement of need and identify outcome indicators by defining what program success means to them. Respect for stakeholder expertise is essential for building rapport with them. The client perspective, which we did not include in our planning, should also be considered, as well as the perspective of other experts (e.g., bringing in a biostatistician to perform a power calculation).

No amount of written documentation or phone conversation can replace the information to be gained from visiting the program in person. My visit to IRC was invaluable in the planning process. We also learned that ongoing communication through multiple modalities can help facilitate the planning process. The planning process should include plans for dissemination. Even within a short timeline, it is useful to propose preliminary and final evaluation reports. Broader dissemination goals, such as publications, should also be discussed during the planning phase.

The evaluator should consider using planning tools during the process, such as a logic model or EPM. As our after-the-fact EPM illustrates, the tools can help guide the discussion on such issues as short-term, intermediate, and long-term outcomes or the process and outcome focus of the evaluation. These questions can be particularly challenging to address in service program environments. This case illustrates the value of a simple tool, namely, keeping an ongoing list of questions to be clarified during the planning process. It is also important to keep in mind that the eventual goal is to produce a written evaluation plan, which itself serves as an important tool.

Conceptual frameworks can be brought in to organize the study variables. During the planning process, theoretical concepts, such as self-efficacy, can be used to frame outcomes. Some service programs are designed using program planning models that incorporate evaluation planning within the framework for overall program planning. Examples of such program planning models in public health include the Precede-Proceed model (Green & Kreuter, 2005) and Intervention Mapping (Bartholomew, Parcel, Kok, & Gottlieb, 2006).

The real nature of the study is shaped during the planning process. Even the purpose of the study should not be articulated prematurely. The goal is to produce an evaluation plan that is as specific as possible, keeping in mind that the procedures cannot be changed once the study has started. The evaluator has to know when to compromise with study design and when such compromise would be counterproductive. Our experience illustrates how a reasonable balance of design rigor and practicalities can be reached on issues such as comparison group, sample size, and data collection burden. Finally, the planning process is not always a linear sequence of steps, such as outlined in the EPIC model. For example, the evaluator cannot understand everything about the context at the first step. Rather, the EPIC model is another tool that helps the evaluator organize the activities and ensure that all important aspects of planning are considered.

CONCLUSION

At the conclusion of the planning process, we were pleased with our evaluation design. We had planned a process and outcome pilot study of the patient navigation service enhancement at IRC. The process component focused on describing the intervention and identifying implementation issues. The process data were to be obtained primarily from the LLS computer system and through informal interviews with IRC staff implementing the patient navigation intervention.

Our outcome study was based on a comparison of callers who received the patient navigation intervention with callers who received the standard IRC service. We had defined specific criteria to determine which callers would qualify for the intervention. Two information specialists were assigned to implement patient navigation, and all qualifying callers whose calls were directed to either of those two staff members were invited to enroll in the intervention. If callers agreed, the information specialists scheduled the intervention, making follow-up calls to participants about a week after the initial contact. The comparison group consisted of qualifying callers whose calls went to any of the other information specialists. We had random assignment because the IRC system already assigns incoming calls to information specialists on a random basis. To capture the outcomes, surveys were mailed to both intervention and comparison group participants 3 weeks after their initial contact with IRC.

Our study design was not perfect because there was the possibility that a difference between the intervention group and the control group could be explained in part by differences in the quality of the information specialists serving the two study groups. However, I was assured by LLS that all information specialists are highly qualified, trained, and experienced, and that there was no plan to assign the most experienced or effective information specialists to the intervention arm. This was a design compromise I decided to accept because having a comparison group and random assignment seemed highly rigorous for a service program pilot study.

REFERENCES

Bandura, A. (1997). *Self-efficacy: The exercise of control.* New York: W. H. Freeman.

Bartholomew, L. K., Parcel, G. S., Kok, G., & Gottlieb, N. H. (2006). *Planning health promotion programs: An intervention mapping approach.* San Francisco: Jossey-Bass.

Centers for Disease Control and Prevention. (1999). Framework for program evaluation in public health. *Morbidity and Mortality Weekly Report, 48*(RR11), 1–40.

Darrow, S. L., Speyer, J., Marcus, A. C., Ter Maat, J., & Krome, D. (1998). Coping with cancer: The impact of the cancer information service on patients and significant others. Part 6. *Journal of Health Communication, 3*(Suppl.), 86–96.

Dohan, D., & Schrag, D. (2005). Using navigators to improve care of underserved patients: Current practices and approaches. *Cancer, 104*(4), 848–855.

Fowler, T., Steakley, C., Garcia, A. R., Kwok, J., & Bennett, L. M. (2006). Reducing disparities in the burden of cancer: The role of patient navigators. *PLoS Medicine, 3*(7), e193.

Freeman, H. P. (2006). Patient navigation: A community based strategy to reduce cancer disparities. *Journal of Urban Health, 83*(2), 139–141.

Freimuth, V. S., Stein, J. A., & Kean, T. J. (1989). *Searching for health information: The cancer information service model.* Philadelphia: University of Pennsylvania Press.

Green, L. W., & Kreuter, M. (2005). *Health program planning: An educational and ecological approach* (4th ed.). New York: McGraw-Hill.

Leukemia & Lymphoma Society. (2004). *Information resource center: Accurate, up-to-date information about leukemia, lymphoma and myeloma* [Brochure]. White Plains, NY: Author.

Leukemia & Lymphoma Society. (2005). *Facts 2005–2006* [Brochure]. White Plains, NY: Author.

McLaughlin, C. P., & Kaluzny, A. D. (1999). *Continuous quality improvement in health care: Theory, implementation, and applications* (2nd ed.). Gaithersburg, MD: Aspen.

Muha, C., Smith, K. S., Baum, S., Ter Maat, J., & Ward, J. A. (1998). The use and selection of sources in information seeking: The cancer information service experience. Part 8. *Journal of Health Communication, 3*(Suppl.), 109–120.

Rutten, L. J., Squiers, L., & Hesse, B. (2006). Cancer-related information seeking: Hints from the 2003 health information national trends survey (HINTS). *Journal of Health Communication, 11*(Suppl. 1), 147–156.

Venn, M. J., Darling, E., Dickens, C., Quine, L., Rutter, D. R., & Slevin, M. L. (1996). The experience and impact of contacting a cancer information service. *European Journal of Cancer Care, 5*(1), 38–42.

Ward, J. A., Baum, S., Ter Maat, J., Thomsen, C. A., & Maibach, E. W. (1998). The value and impact of the cancer information service telephone service. Part 4. *Journal of Health Communication, 3*(Suppl.), 50–70.

5

CALL AND RESPONSE: DEVELOPING A COLLABORATIVE EVALUATION PLAN FOR A NEW COMMUNITY-BASED PROGRAM

Thomas M. Reischl and Susan P. Franzen

For more than 5 years, we have been collaborating with a group of organizations in the greater Flint, Michigan, community to improve maternal and child health services. Our work on these efforts has included needs assessment and program evaluation, while our partner organizations have focused on service provision, systems development, and patient education/engagement. In this chapter, we describe our relationship with partner organizations and how we developed a set of program evaluation methods to study the implementation and some initial outcomes of a new community-based program that was planned, developed, and implemented during this period.

Writing this chapter gave us the opportunity to reflect on how program evaluations need to be responsive not only to the specific goals of the program, but also to the evolution of a program, especially during its early development. Robert Stake (2004a, 2004b) has argued that program evaluators should adopt a "responsive predisposition" that focuses attention on key issues, problems, and concerns experienced by the program's stakeholders. Stake (2004b) writes, "It is common for the design of a study to develop slowly, with continuing adaption of design and data gathering passed to the evaluators' growing acquaintance with program activity, stakeholder aspiration, and social and political contexts" (p. 209).

Daniel Stufflebeam (2001) applies the label "client-centered studies" to Stake's and similar evaluation models, suggesting that being responsive is akin to working with and for clients (stakeholders)—those responsible for funding or implementing a program. Responsive or client-centered evaluations engage the people involved in program delivery and help them evaluate the program and use the evaluation findings to improve the program. Being responsive or client-centered requires improvisation on the part of the evaluator. One cannot be responsive if there are set criteria or established evaluation plans before a program is developed. The risk of the client-centered approach is that program implementers will not be held accountable by reasonable external standards. Also, the program funders and implementers must be receptive to an open and flexible evaluation plan and to a planning process that addresses the concerns of a broad group of stakeholders. This approach requires a level of trust and patience among partners and an appreciation for ambiguity (Stufflebeam & Shinkfield, 2007).

We titled this chapter "Call and Response" for several reasons. This phrase is used to describe a traditional and improvisational rhetorical form that originated in sub-Saharan African cultures and was brought to the New World by African slaves. Call and response is used for civic discussions, religious rituals, and storytelling, and also in musical expression. It is characterized by "spontaneous verbal and nonverbal interaction between speaker and listener in which all of the statements ('calls') are punctuated by expressions ('responses') from the listener" (Smitherman, 1977, p. 104). The listeners are just as responsible as the speakers for expressing and interpreting the intended message. Call and response is an apt metaphor for the client-centered approach we took in developing the evaluation plan for a new intervention. We did not begin our involvement in this project with a specific set of evaluation plans. Instead, we committed to help with the program planning and to develop an evaluation study that was responsive to the goals of the new program. We also like this metaphor because it honors the historical and cultural traditions of the new intervention's focus population: African American families. Finally, the title reflects the nature of the services provided by the program that we evaluated; the new program was an information and referral service that was delivered primarily over the telephone. The families in need called and the program staff responded.

Our involvement required a great deal of improvisation as we revised the evaluation plans over the course of the project. The new program tried a number of strategies to engage a variety of partner organizations, including substantial involvement from three community-based organizations (CBOs). Each new step in the program's development represented the "call," and our efforts to shape the development of the evaluation to best document the program's implementation and outcomes were the "response."

GUIDING PRINCIPLES

We were committed to developing the study's procedures in collaboration with the program staff and other community stakeholders who were interested in monitoring program implementation and outcomes. This new program and its evaluation study were adopted as a core project by the Genesee County Community Board of the Prevention Research Center of Michigan (PRC/MI). As a core project, staff working on the project must commit to a set of community-based public health principles (Schulz, Israel, Selig, Bayer, & Griffin, 1998) that emphasize the importance of collaborating with CBOs, public health agencies, and educational institutions in all major phases of the research process (defining the problem, gathering data, interpreting results, and disseminating findings) and of ensuring that the research products and outcomes benefit the community where the study is conducted.

We were also committed to the program evaluation standards adopted by the American Evaluation Association (Joint Committee on Standards for Educational Evaluation, 1994). These standards embrace the importance of the study's *utility* to all stakeholders involved or affected by the evaluation. The utility standard requires evaluation methods to be responsive to stakeholder needs; to be forthright about fundamental values; and to ensure access to clear, timely, and useful evaluation reports. The standards also include a commitment to conduct *feasible* studies that are realistic, diplomatic, prudent, and frugal so that the procedures employed minimize program disruptions, produce results of sufficient value, mobilize political support, and are cost-effective. The *propriety* standards ensure that evaluations are conducted legally, ethically, and with regard for the welfare of those involved and affected by the evaluation study. The University of Michigan Health Sciences Institutional Review Board (IRB) approved and annually reviewed the evaluation research procedures involving human subjects. The *accuracy* standards promote procedures that reveal and convey the most technically adequate information about the merit of the program being evaluated. The methods used should produce accurate information about the program itself and the context in which the program exists and maximize the use of reliable and valid data collection and data analysis procedures. Finally, the reports of the results should be explicitly justified and guard against distortion caused by personal biases.

BACKGROUND OF A COMMUNITY-BASED PROGRAM

The impetus for the program was a request for proposals (RFP) from the Health Resources and Services Administration (HRSA) of the U.S. Department of Health and Human Services (DHHS) in April 2004 that directed applicants to develop pilot programs to reduce infant mortality among African Americans by preventing low birth weight, preterm births, and sudden infant death syndrome (SIDS). The pilot programs could also address other causes or factors associated with disparately higher rates of infant mortality among African Americans. Other requirements included using evidence-based interventions, attending to cultural competence and quality, building on other DHHS-funded programs, and using an advisor group that included representatives from other DHHS-funded programs and other stakeholders key to designing and implementing the pilot program. The RFP identified four states eligible for this funding: Illinois, Michigan, Mississippi, and South Carolina. The grant would support a pilot program for 4 years in a local community with high numbers of African American infant deaths.

Key Stakeholders

The Michigan Department of Community Health (MDCH) took primary responsibility for writing the proposal and approached local agencies and organizations in the City of Flint (Genesee County) to solicit their interest. MDCH staff asked the Greater Flint Health Coalition (GFHC) to take a lead role in convening organizations and stakeholders and coordinating the implementation of the pilot program in Flint and surrounding Genesee County. The organization chart in Figure 5.1 illustrates the relationships between key stakeholders for this program after the initial planning meetings.

MDCH served as the administrative agency with primary responsibility for submitting reports to HRSA. MDCH is responsible for health policy and management of the state's publicly funded health service systems. According to its Web site, GFHC is a

> non-profit 501(c)3 organization whose mission is to improve the health status of Genesee County residents and to improve the quality and cost-effectiveness of the health care delivery system. It is both a community/institutional partnership and multifaceted collaboration, with a board that is a broad reflection of the community's leadership—including government, hospitals, labor, business, insurers, physicians, education, consumers and the faith-based community (2005).

At the time this program began, GFHC supported activities to address health care quality, access, and costs with specific programs addressing back

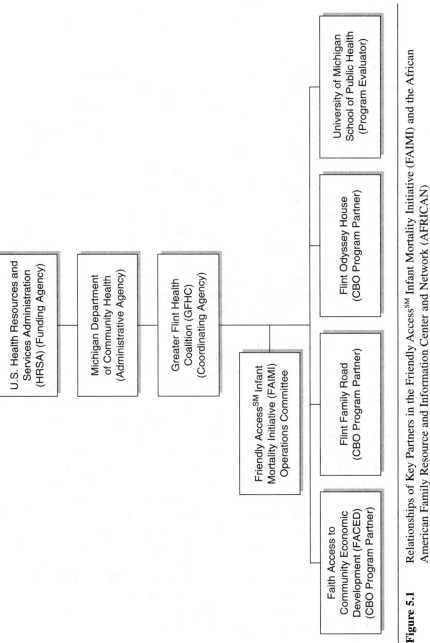

Figure 5.1   Relationships of Key Partners in the Friendly Access^{SM} Infant Mortality Initiative (FAIMI) and the African American Family Resource and Information Center and Network (AFRICAN)

pain management, heart failure care practices, maternal and child health care, diabetes testing and monitoring, mental health and substance use, pharmacy practices, health care workforce development, and racial and ethnic disparities in health and health care.

MDCH approached GFHC to coordinate this program because of the broad composition of its board members, which included key leaders in the health care and business community. GFHC was also coordinating the 5-year Flint/Genesee County Friendly Access[SM] Project[1] to improve maternal and child health care services and participated in a number of collaborative efforts to reduce infant mortality in Genesee County. MDCH asked GFHC to convene partner organizations and to work with the MDCH grant writer to produce a proposal responding to the RFP.

The key stakeholders involved in developing a plan and a proposal represented organizations that deliver a variety of maternal and child health services in Flint and in Genesee County, Michigan. Many of the representatives of stakeholder organizations involved in planning the new program eventually agreed to serve on the program's Operations Committee. The Operations Committee initially met every 2 weeks and later met monthly. The committee members provided advice and guidance to GFHC, the three CBOs who became program partners, and the program evaluators.

Planning the New Program

After the larger group of stakeholders outlined the initial ideas for the program, GFHC invited three CBOs to play leadership roles in developing and implementing the program because of their extensive experience serving African American clients. One CBO, Flint Family Road, offered a variety of health, social, and human services to promote healthy eating (especially for pregnant women and infants), employment opportunities, money management, stress management, parenting skills, and substance use prevention. Another CBO, Faith Access to Community Economic Development (FACED), was a key partner in a variety of maternal and child health initiatives and facilitated the activities of faith-based initiatives such as Faith Based Health Teams and tobacco-use reduction projects in more than 50 congregations in Genesee County. The third CBO, the Flint Odyssey House, Inc., Health Awareness Center, promotes holistic health and human services with an emphasis on preventing infant mortality, HIV/AIDS, sexually transmitted diseases (STDs), tuberculosis, diabetes, and lead poisoning through teaching African and African American history and culture and promoting positive racial/ethnic identity and health behaviors.

The outcomes of the planning meetings included a plan for developing a new collaborative initiative with many of the partner organizations already engaged in the Flint/Genesee County Friendly Access Project. The new initiative was called the Friendly Access Infant Mortality Initiative (FAIMI). One of FAIMI's goals was to develop and deliver an information and referral service that focused on the health and human services needs of African American families, especially families with young children and women of childbearing age. The new information and referral service would be the primary component of the larger program's efforts to help coordinate and integrate health and human services to better serve African American women and families. The larger goals were to reduce low birth weight, premature births and infant deaths among African American women. More specific objectives included the following:

- Increasing the percentage of African American parents receiving parental education in the area of infant safety
- Increasing the number of African American women practicing appropriate health behaviors before, during, and after pregnancy
- Increasing the percentage of African American women receiving early, continuous, and adequate prenatal care
- Reducing the number of unintended pregnancies in the African American population

New Program Characteristics

The new information and referral service was eventually named the African American Family Resource Information Center and Network (AFRICAN). AFRICAN was a telephone referral service with the local phone number A-F-R-I-C-A-N (237-4226) and trained telephone service providers called community navigators. AFRICAN's operations were based at the GFHC offices, but three of the community navigators were employed by and based at the three partner CBOs (Flint Family Road, FACED, and Flint Odyssey House). The role of the community navigators was to assist clients in navigating the myriad health and human services available in Genesee County. The community navigators were trained to assess clients' service needs and refer them to services that addressed their needs. The community navigators also assisted in developing a community health and human services "systems map" that catalogued and described community services and their intended clients.

The development of the AFRICAN telephone referral service intentionally focused on the shared responsibility of GFHC and the three CBOs. While GFHC employed the program's director and lead community navigator, the three partner CBOs each received subcontracts to employ a part-time program supervisor and a part-time community navigator. The CBOs' community navigators were called "decentralized" navigators, because they provided the telephone information and referral service from the CBOs' service sites instead of from the central program office at GFHC. The CBOs' program supervisors also agreed to serve on an administrative committee with GFHC staff called the AFRICAN Task Force that initially met twice a month to discuss program administration issues. The goals of this arrangement were to promote the visibility of the AFRICAN service at community organizations with extensive experience serving African American families, enhance the CBOs' capacity to collaborate with larger health and human services organizations, and enhance the sustainability of the program in the community.

Because the community navigators work at the central office and at decentralized sites, they used a Web-based management information system to record information about every client, including information needs assessments, family background information, and referrals made during the call. The service was marketed to African American families in Flint and surrounding Genesee County, but all clients (regardless of race or ethnicity) received services. The community navigators began receiving calls to AFRICAN in August 2005.

The AFRICAN navigators assisted callers and also conducted outreach visits to community health clinics and human services organizations to recruit clients. When the navigator contacted a client (by telephone or face to face), the navigator conducted an extensive intake and service provision interview. The interview protocol included questions about the client's contact information, demographics and family background, pregnancy status, how the client learned about AFRICAN services, the client's service needs (e.g., housing, health insurance, pregnancy support), and initial referrals made to address the client's service needs. The interview data were entered into the Web-based information system during or immediately after the service interview.

AFRICAN staff also met with community health and human services providers on a regular basis to market the new service. The program staff described the AFRICAN service to service providers and encouraged them to tell their clients about the service. The program staff also left bundles of brochures about AFRICAN with the service providers.

Finally, AFRICAN staff met with specific human service providers to discuss how to address emerging barriers for AFRICAN clients. For example, when free or low-cost disposable diapers were no longer available at a particular community service agency, AFRICAN staff called another community agency to ask if they could provide this service. They addressed similar emerging needs when a home fuel assistance program lost its funding and when new regulations were established for women applying for Women, Infants, and Children (WIC) services. These efforts were directed at streamlining the health and human service systems to provide more effective services for women and young children.

The long-term or distal outcomes for this program focused on reducing infant mortality by reducing low birth weight, premature births, and SIDS, whereas the short-term or proximal outcomes focused on helping clients successfully navigate the complicated health and human services system to receive the health care and the parenting support they needed to have healthy pregnancies and healthy infants. The program's theory of action suggested that the following activities would lead to these outcomes:

- Engaging health and human services providers in planning processes and networking
- Recruiting AFRICAN clients through social marketing and outreach
- Providing access to a telephone information and referral service that could quickly identify service needs and make appropriate referrals to health and human services providers

Planning the Evaluation Study

Because of our experience conducting needs assessments and evaluation studies, GFHC invited us to attend the initial grant-writing meetings to assist with developing a feasible evaluation plan. The budget for this program included a subcontract for program evaluation services (provided by the University of Michigan) approximately equal to $43,000 per year, or about 10% of the total program operation costs. We were involved in all program planning activities and served as a voting member on the FAIMI Operations Committee and on the AFRICAN Task Force. Below we summarize the development and implementation of the evaluation study design for this program following the Evaluation Planning Incorporating Context (EPIC) model.

ASSESS CONTEXT

Understand the Organizational and Political Environment

Assessing the organizational and political environment for this program required attention at several levels. At a national level, concern is growing about high rates of infant mortality in the United States, especially the higher rates among African Americans. Though the infant mortality rate in the United States has been falling, it remains the second highest recorded rate among industrialized nations (DHHS, 2004). In Michigan, there are parallel concerns about the effects of lost manufacturing jobs on the health of the state's citizens, including an infant mortality rate that is higher than the national rate. Nowhere are the effects of lost manufacturing jobs more pronounced than in Flint and surrounding communities. Since 1970, more than 60,000 automobile manufacturing jobs have been eliminated in and around Flint. The infant mortality rate in Genesee County is the highest (11.2 deaths per 1,000 live births averaged over 2002 to 2006) among the higher-populated counties in the state (Michigan Department of Community Health, 2007). Within Flint and surrounding Genesee County, there has been a growing concern about racial and ethnic disparities in health problems, especially infant mortality. The 2000 U.S. Decennial Census noted that among the 124,943 people living in Flint, 53.3% were African American and 41.4% were White.

The AFRICAN information and referral service operated as a partnership between GFHC and three CBOs that provided a variety of human services to African American families. The decentralized community navigators were hired and supervised by the three CBOs. Sharing the responsibility for implementing AFRICAN required effective coordination among GFHC and the three CBOs. All four organizations had been partners since 1999 in a collaborative effort funded by the Centers for Disease Control and Prevention (CDC) called Racial and Ethnic Approaches to Community Health (REACH) 2010 (CDC, 2007). The REACH 2010 initiative also addressed high levels of infant mortality among African American women with population-focused interventions that embody cultural understanding, sensitivity, and relevance. The project initiated a variety of education and support programs for at-risk families and implemented professional training and media campaigns to raise awareness about racism and racial disparities in infant mortality rates and to help reduce these disparities.

Despite their history of working together, GFHC and the three CBOs faced a number of coordination challenges during initial development of the AFRICAN program. There were disagreements about the appropriate job qualifications for the decentralized community navigators hired at the CBOs and about who was responsible for coordinating their work hours and work settings. GFHC focused on coordinating the training and work hours of all community navigators, while the CBOs wanted to have more power in determining the work hours of the decentralized navigators under their supervision. While these problems were being addressed during the difficult start-up period of a new program, there was considerable pressure from the state administrative agency (MDCH) to have a program up and running. The delays in the program's initial development also resulted in delays in developing an evaluation plan and starting evaluation activities. As we describe below, our role as evaluators in this effort often put us in the middle of some of the interorganizational conflicts.

Define the Relationship Between the Evaluator and the Sponsor

Our relationship with GFHC and the three CBOs had been established through partnerships on previous projects. GFHC, two of the three CBOs, and the University of Michigan had been institutional partners on a Genesee County Community Advisory Board for the PRC/MI since 1998. GFHC had invited us to conduct needs assessment and evaluation services on a previous project, the Flint/Genesee County Friendly Access Project, that engaged area health service providers in activities to improve maternal and child health services in Genesee County. We conducted two large baseline survey studies that involved interviewing women ($n = 358$) who had just given birth about their experiences with the perinatal health services they received and interviewing parents or guardians ($n = 377$) who had brought their children to pediatric health clinics about their experiences with receiving the pediatric health services. Using these data sets, we wrote needs assessment reports for perinatal and pediatric health services and reports comparing the experiences of African American and White (European American) patients. These baseline data sets were useful when planning the development and evaluation of the AFRICAN information and referral service. GFHC, noting the continuity between the Friendly Access Project and the current program, named the new program the Friendly Access Infant Mortality Initiative (FAIMI) of which the AFRICAN information and referral service was one program activity.

GFHC subcontracted with PRC/MI at the University of Michigan to develop and implement an evaluation study of AFRICAN services. As part of the subcontract agreement, GFHC also requested that the lead evaluator serve as a voting member on two program advisory and coordinating committees related to this program: the FAIMI Operations Committee and the AFRICAN Task Force. Given the potential conflicts of interest that may arise from such a relationship to the program's leadership, we asked GFHC and the other partners if they were comfortable with the evaluator having voting privileges on these two committees. In our brief discussion of this issue, they expressed confidence that any potential conflicts of interest caused by playing a dual role of collaborator and evaluator could be reasonably resolved. Over the 4-year span of this program, the lead evaluator remained on these committees, participating in nearly all important discussions regarding developing and supervising AFRICAN. Despite having played a role in implementing the program, we cannot recall any occasions when we experienced a conflict of interest or any unusual tension created by the dual role played in implementing and evaluating this program.

On the contrary, playing a dual role may have enhanced the other partners' awareness and engagement in developing and implementing the evaluation work plan. For example, we presented updates on the evaluation work plan and evaluation activities at nearly every meeting of the two committees, and we asked the committee members to comment and provide suggestions on the planned evaluation activities. We also shared early drafts of data collection tools and evaluation reports and solicited suggestions. We incorporated every reasonable suggestion and provided explanations when a suggestion was infeasible or contrary to the goals of the evaluation studies. As such, we considered our relationship to the sponsor and other stakeholders to be "collaborative"; we conducted all of the evaluation work, but we reported to the committees and the coordinating agency (GFHC) and solicited suggestions for improving the evaluation plans, activities, results, and final products.

Determine the Level of the Evaluation

Because we focused on the development and effects of the AFRICAN service in one community, the focus of this evaluation study was on the program level (implementation issues) and on the individual level (client outcomes). At the program level, the evaluation activities focused on program implementation, including how well AFRICAN reached the intended population for these services, addressed relevant problems of the program's clients, and provided information and referrals to a variety of community health and human service providers. At the client level, the evaluation activities focused on the clients' reported experiences with AFRICAN services and with the health and human services they received in the community.

GATHER RECONNAISSANCE

Specify Evaluation Uses

Early in the planning phases of AFRICAN, it became clear to us that tracking and monitoring program implementation would be a primary use of the evaluation findings. The project had to be built from scratch. The program implementers worked with the suggestions provided by a variety of stakeholders and collaborators, but they also needed reliable and authentic assessment of project activities to understand how their program worked and how to improve its capacity and reach. Therefore, the program needed accurate assessments of the number of new clients who used the AFRICAN services each month, why they were accessing AFRICAN, and the referrals that were provided to new clients. We presented the plan for collecting program implementation indicators to the coordinating agency (GFHC), the Operations Committee, and the AFRICAN Task Force and argued that evaluation data on implementation would help them monitor the development of the new program and identify how well AFRICAN was marketing its services to the intended population of concern: African American women who were pregnant or had a young child. We received input that AFRICAN was intended for a wider audience of African American families, because family members often play a key role in supporting pregnant women or women with young children and could be seeking information and referrals for the young women or children.

After the project was developed, the staff trained, and most of the wrinkles ironed out, the program staff and other stakeholders were interested in assessing how well AFRICAN was meeting its goals. Were they delivering a service that was appreciated by the clients being served? Were the clients being referred to the appropriate services? Were the clients successful in receiving prenatal or pediatric health care services that could ensure healthy pregnancies and healthy infants? They were also interested in knowing whether AFRICAN played a role in reducing infant mortality rates among African American women.

Validate Perspectives

Because we had collaborated with nearly all the stakeholders involved in this project on a previous project (Friendly Access), it was not difficult to discern and validate the sponsor's intentions for the evaluation study. The RFP required that evaluation activity be included in program proposals.

MDCH trusted GFHC's decision to invite us to provide the evaluation services. It appeared that the other partners and stakeholders also trusted the choice of the University of Michigan evaluation research team. We also believe that the partners trusted our involvement in the program because we had been collaborating on other projects for more than 5 years.

As explained above, we also invited comments on our plans and activities from MDCH, GFHC, and other stakeholders as part of our commitment to collaborate in all evaluation activities. Early in the planning process, the GFHC leadership expressed at a planning meeting of partners and stakeholders their hope that the evaluators would "hold their feet to the fire" and provide both positive and negative feedback to the planning committees and to the program staff.

Progress reports on evaluation activities were included on the agendas of every planning committee meeting. Program staff members were eager to share evaluation reports with planning committees as soon as they were submitted. The evaluators were invited to provide formal presentations of preliminary and final reports. The evaluation sponsors were happy to use the results of the evaluation studies to improve their program.

ENGAGE STAKEHOLDERS

Identify and Invite Stakeholders

Because of its infrastructure and capacity, GFHC assumed responsibility for identifying and convening program partners and other stakeholders for the development of the AFRICAN project and the evaluation study. GFHC staff were well positioned to convene the key stakeholders because of their larger coordinating role in Genesee County. Serving on the GFHC board, for example, were state and local lawmakers and executives from the county's health department, health care systems, chamber of commerce, large industries, labor unions, health care payer corporations, medical societies, school districts, universities, and human service organizations.

GFHC was also responsible for engaging key stakeholders over the course of the program. The first year of the program focused on planning with the CBOs and other key stakeholders. GFHC established an Operations Committee to work with program staff to accomplish the planning goals. This committee met twice a month for the first year of the program and once a month thereafter. When the program initiated the AFRICAN information and referral services in the second year, GFHC established a smaller working group called the AFRICAN Task Force, which included the GFHC program staff, leaders from the three partner CBOs, and the lead evaluator. The Task Force also met twice a month initially and then once a month for the duration of the program.

Define Stakeholder Roles and Structure for Their Input

As explained previously, the lead evaluator played a dual role, serving on advisory committees and evaluating the program. The coordinating agency (GFHC) asked him to serve on all planning committees, comment on the development of program operations, and vote on key decisions. He was also expected to lead an evaluation study that would provide accurate, useful, and unbiased reports on the program's progress and outcomes. The tension created by the dual role may be a natural consequence of being committed to the principles of community-based public health research. When the evaluator commits to a collaborative and mutually beneficial partnership with other program stakeholders, there is a risk that maintaining the partnership may take priority over the ethical obligation of freely and accurately reporting evaluation results. Sharing this concern with GFHC staff and other members of the Operations Committee and AFRICAN Task Force was one way to address the potential problems of playing a dual role.

We hoped the discussion would encourage all stakeholders to acknowledge the potential issues, share in the responsibility of addressing potential problems, and understand the value of producing evaluation studies that could be viewed credibly as accurate and unbiased. We believed that developing evaluation plans in response to the developing program plans would help the stakeholders understand and value the evaluators' work, and they would not be surprised if any of the evaluation reports revealed the need for program improvements. After all stakeholders reviewed the evaluation plans, we felt confident that implementing the evaluation studies as planned would keep our focus on producing the most accurate reports possible.

Another challenge was that the lead evaluator was viewed as an outsider. He did not live or work in Flint or Genesee County (he lived in Ann Arbor and worked for the University of Michigan), he was not African American, and he had not experienced the barriers that racial and ethnic minorities often experience. He did not feel like he was "part of the community," and we believe that other stakeholders viewed him as an outsider as well. Many of the stakeholders were aware of past "abuses" of power by university-based researchers who took advantage of opportunities to conduct research in community settings without long-term benefit to the host community. We were aware of the perception that university researchers are often arrogant about the value of their own ideas. As an outsider, the lead evaluator was cautious about expressing ideas and opinions, especially on issues where the "insiders" disagreed, and understood that stepping over the line with a strong opinion could be viewed as intrusive or insensitive.

Serving on the Operations Committee and the AFRICAN Task Force, we had to acknowledge the lead evaluator's outsider status and explore with the other stakeholders the best way for the lead evaluator to be helpful to them. We found several general principles that helped:

1. *Be an active listener.* When discussions reveal a problem or a disagreement, it is important to listen intently to the views expressed. Record or remember not only the ideas but key phrases used by various speakers. There may be an opportunity for the active listener to accurately summarize the views being expressed using their own words, which could help the group see a solution or a compromise. Demonstrating skill in active listening can also affirm the evaluator's value as a thoughtful and responsive contributor to the group's work.

2. *Be tolerant of disagreement and conflict.* It is often important for stakeholders to express their diverging goals and values as they address the operational problems of running a program. Moving a group to a solution too quickly may prevent stakeholders from expressing important goals and values and keep them from understanding each other's perspectives. A fuller understanding of all stakeholders will be an asset for building stronger partnerships and for future problem solving.

3. *Acknowledge your "outsider" status.* Before expressing an idea or offering a summary of the discussion, preface your statement with a polite and intentional acknowledgment of your outsider status; for example, "I may be speaking out of turn, but . . ." or "I realize I am an outsider here, but . . ." Starting your statement with a disclaimer may rhetorically weaken the statement, but it may allow the "insiders" to be open to your ideas and opinions.

Establish Group Processes for Ongoing Stakeholder Input

Because of the commitment of the program's sponsor, partners, and stakeholders to meet at least monthly, the evaluation team had ample opportunities to meet face to face and discuss the development and implementation of evaluation study activities and evaluation reports. Initially, we presented proposals for evaluation plans and procedures. Meeting participants provided suggestions for refining the procedures. Evaluation reports were distributed by mail and discussed at meetings three to four times a year. We also maintained regular telephone and e-mail contact with the program's sponsor to ensure that expectations were being met regarding the development and implementation of the evaluation plans.

DESCRIBE THE PROGRAM

FAIMI and its project AFRICAN were new interventions. The development of the evaluation plan occurred in tandem with the development of the new interventions in the early phases of this grant-funded effort. In this section, we describe how we learned about the development of the new interventions so we could develop evaluation plans to describe AFRICAN's implementation and examine its outcomes.

We learned about the development of FAIMI and AFRICAN by meeting with program partners and reviewing the plans being developed by program staff at GFHC. The initial planning meetings began in June 2004 when GFHC convened community stakeholders interested in responding to the HRSA request for proposals. Beginning in June 2005, when the final operations of AFRICAN were being planned and community navigators were being trained, GFHC convened meetings with a new committee, the AFRICAN Task Force, made up of GFHC staff, supervisory staff from the three partner CBOs, and the lead evaluator from the University of Michigan. At this time and for the duration of the program, the FAIMI Operations Committee and the AFRICAN Task Force began meeting once a month. AFRICAN started working with new clients in August 2005.

During these bimonthly committee meetings (recorded in detailed meeting minutes by GFHC staff), we learned about the program staff's plans and activities (described in detail above). We also presented initial plans for evaluation activities to members of these committees and received their input.

FOCUS THE EVALUATION

With a limited budget for the evaluation activities, we needed to establish procedures that would take advantage of existing data sources and focus on key evaluation questions. One example was the AFRICAN call center data records. AFRICAN staff had created a Web-based information system for all clients, and we proposed including data fields in this system that would help us accurately describe the population served, the service needs of the client population, and the number and nature of client referrals. Another example was the existence of data from recent studies of large and demographically similar samples of clients in Genesee County who rated the quality of prenatal and pediatric health care. Having such data collected within the previous 2 years allowed us to have a comparison group design without having to collect additional data.

With limits on available data sets, we needed to consider which evaluation questions could be adequately addressed in this study. An evaluation planning matrix (EPM) illustrates the range of evaluation questions, measures, and data sources considered for this study (see Table 5.1). At the time the proposal was submitted, the proposal committee had outlined several areas of concern for the evaluation team. The stakeholders wanted to know how well AFRICAN reached the intended population for services, addressed relevant problems of the program's clients, and provided referrals to community health and human services providers. The overarching goal of the program was to reduce infant mortality.

At the beginning of the program, we held additional meetings with AFRICAN staff to help determine how to quantify the research questions. At the meetings, we noted that many of the research questions listed in the EPM could be answered if the AFRICAN staff went through a specific protocol with each client and if the evaluation team had access to the call center records (for secondary data analyses). To get clients' perceptions of the program, we would need to interview or survey the clients (primary data collection). To assess the program's impact on infant mortality, we would need to consult with MDCH, the agency responsible for producing Genesee County's infant mortality statistics (secondary data analyses).

Given the historically negative relationship of African Americans, research, and health care (Brandon, Isaac, & LaVeist, 2005; Cook, Selig, Wedge, & Gohn-Baube, 1999), we recognized the need to minimize the data collection burden on the clients. The stakeholders agreed that the AFRICAN call records would be a primary source of data on client demographics, client needs, and program referrals. Additionally, the stakeholders agreed that the evaluation plan should include interviews with clients who were most likely to be members of the community of concern (i.e., pregnant women and caregivers of children under 2 years of age).

We needed to look at the evaluation plan to ensure that the evaluation questions could be answered using the proposed methodologies in a cost-effective manner. We also needed to look for areas where we could "piggyback" on existing research. The committee members acknowledged that,

(Text continues on page 110)

Table 5.1 Evaluation Planning Matrix for the AFRICAN Evaluation Study

Evaluation Questions	Process Evaluation			Short-Term Outcomes			Long-Term Outcomes		
	Outcomes	Data Sources	Data Elements	Outcomes	Data Sources	Data Elements	Outcomes	Data Sources	Data Elements
Service Population									
What population do we serve?	Demographics of call center clients	Call center records	Age, race, gender, transportation, employment, education, pregnancy, weeks pregnant, number of children						
Did the program reach the intended population?	Demographics from call center clients would match program focus	Call center records	Age, race, gender, transportation, employment, education, pregnancy, weeks pregnant, number of children	Demographics from call center clients would match program focus	Call center records	Age, race, gender, transportation, employment, education, pregnancy, weeks pregnant, number of children			
How many calls are coming in a month? A year?	Counts of clients	Call center records	Counts of clients	Counts of clients meets goal	Call center records	Counts of clients meets goal			

(Continued)

105

Table 5.1 (Continued)

Evaluation Questions	Process Evaluation			Short-Term Outcomes			Long-Term Outcomes		
	Outcomes	Data Sources	Data Elements	Outcomes	Data Sources	Data Elements	Outcomes	Data Sources	Data Elements
What are the varieties of problems facing pregnant women?	Analysis of clients' needs	Call center records	Records of reason for call						
What type of problem is most reported?	Frequencies of reason for call	Call center records	Records of reason for call						
Services Provided									
How many referrals are made in a month? A year?	Counts of referrals	Call center records	Counts of clients	Counts of referrals meets goal	Call center records	Counts of referrals meets goal			
What service providers were referrals made to?	Frequencies of referrals	Call center records							

Evaluation Questions	Process Evaluation			Short-Term Outcomes			Long-Term Outcomes		
	Outcomes	Data Sources	Data Elements	Outcomes	Data Sources	Data Elements	Outcomes	Data Sources	Data Elements
Are the referrals helpful to the clients? Are appropriate referrals provided?				Clients report referrals helpful and appropriate	Interviews	Questions asking clients about referrals			
How well did the program address the relevant issues of the program clients?									
Are some service providers nonresponsive?				Clients report agencies nonresponsive	Interviews	Questions asking clients if service providers helped them in a timely manner			

(Continued)

Table 5.1 (Continued)

Evaluation Questions	Process Evaluation			Short-Term Outcomes			Long-Term Outcomes		
	Outcomes	Data Sources	Data Elements	Outcomes	Data Sources	Data Elements	Outcomes	Data Sources	Data Elements
Do the clients contact the service providers?				Clients report they contacted the referrals	Interviews	Questions asking clients about referrals			
Are the clients satisfied with the way the AFRICAN treated them?				Clients report satisfaction	Interviews	Questions asking clients about satisfaction			
Social Marketing									
Is there a relationship between call center volume and social marketing techniques?	Analysis—Crosstabs—Counts of clients by social marketing techniques at the time of call	Call center records	Records of marketing efforts, frequencies of clients						
How did the client hear about the program?	Counts of responses	Call center records	Questions asking clients how they heard about the program						

Evaluation Questions	Process Evaluation			Short-Term Outcomes			Long-Term Outcomes		
	Outcomes	Data Sources	Data Elements	Outcomes	Data Sources	Data Elements	Outcomes	Data Sources	Data Elements
Relationships With Health Care Providers									
Were the clients satisfied with their pediatricians?				Clients indicate satisfaction	Interviews	Reference Friendly Access questions asking clients about pediatric satisfaction			
Were the clients satisfied with their prenatal doctors?				Clients indicate satisfaction	Interviews	Reference Friendly Access questions asking clients about prenatal satisfaction			
Infant Mortality Trends									
Are infant mortality rates in Genesee County lower after the program?							Lower infant mortality rates	MDCH	Infant mortality rates

because of the high rate of infant mortality in Genesee County, many programs in the county were focused on reducing infant mortality. The AFRICAN stakeholders acknowledged that the program was designed to work in tandem with existing community infant mortality reduction initiatives. If infant mortality decreased in Genesee County, AFRICAN could not take sole credit for any decrease. At best, the credit would have to be shared with other infant mortality programs. Thus, the evaluation plan did not need to focus on infant mortality statistics.

Because of proper planning at the proposal stage, we had budgeted for secondary analysis of the AFRICAN call center records and interviews with a sample of clients. We had to design a data collection protocol that fit within the budget and answered the most research questions possible using the methods prescribed. Some of the questions the committees wanted to address could not be answered using our methodologies. Other questions had to be dropped out of concern for client privacy or excessive time burden on the clients.

As we started building the evaluation tools, we focused on the three broad questions for this evaluation and started generating more specific questions that could be addressed by the evaluation study:

1. *How well did AFRICAN reach the intended population for services?* What population do we serve? Did the program reach the intended population? How many calls are coming in a month? A year? How many referrals are given in a month? A year?

2. *How well did AFRICAN address relevant problems of the program's clients?* What are the varieties of problems facing pregnant women? What type of problem is most reported? Are the referrals helpful to the clients? Are some service providers nonresponsive?

3. *How well did AFRICAN provide referrals to community health and human services providers?* Are appropriate referrals provided? To what service providers were referrals made? Did the clients contact the service providers? Are the clients satisfied with the way the AFRICAN staff members treated them?

We also included methods to address two research questions related to desired program outcomes: were the clients satisfied with their pediatricians and were the clients satisfied with their prenatal doctors? While the AFRICAN services had little control over the delivery of health care services, the community navigators were hoping to improve clients' experiences with health and human services providers. Another reason we included methods to assess the experience of health care services was that we had strong baseline data from large and representative samples of new mothers and parents (caregivers) of young children from the earlier collaborative evaluation of the Friendly Access Project. These questions were of interest to the GFHC FAIMI staff and the evaluators. Another outcome question (Are infant mortality rates lower after the program?) was important to all of the stakeholders and would be addressed using the MDCH infant mortality data. We deemed these three questions "high priority" and included them in further evaluation plans.

The call center records (e.g., demographics, needs of clients, number of referrals) answered many of the questions identified by the stakeholders and listed in the EPM. For instance, we could answer the question "Did the program reach the intended population?" by comparing the demographic statistics we gathered from the call center records to the profile of the individuals we were trying to reach with the program.

Some questions could be answered easily by asking clients their opinions and experiences in an interview (client satisfaction with services). Other questions were too broad and could not be translated into our research design. For example, we could correlate the type of media (e.g., television, radio) used to advertise the program and the number of calls received by AFRICAN each month (Is there a relationship between call center volume and social marketing techniques?), but we could not use that information to answer the question "What is the most effective way of social marketing the program?" For instance, we noticed an association between AFRICAN running television ads and the number of new callers, but confounders may have been responsible for the increase in call volume. Another stream of questions (Are there other programs addressing these issues? Why aren't women accessing them? Do women know how to navigate the "system"?) required different methodologies and did not fall into our broad evaluation objectives; thus, they were not pursued in our evaluation.

Assess Potential Data Collection Burden

We had narrowed our list of research questions and considered budgetary concerns, but we still needed to consider the potential burden inflicted on AFRICAN staff and clients by our evaluation plans. We had to be sensitive to the fact that clients would be calling in because they needed help with a problem and may not have the time to provide other information helpful to the evaluation study. Also clients might have privacy concerns and be unwilling to provide personal information over the telephone during an initial call. Thus, we decided to collect a minimal amount of demographic data during the client's first call to AFRICAN. We also decided to contact and interview a selected subset of clients after the initial call and collect more information.

Putting Together the Wish List (Part I)

We needed two systems for collecting data. One system was needed to collect client data, including the demographics of the person calling (or walking into a decentralized location) (e.g., gender, age, address, phone number, pregnancy status, employment status), type of need (e.g., baby items, medical referrals, pregnancy needs, help with bills), and to what service providers the client was referred. A second system was needed to collect and store information from client interviews we conducted.

For the first system, we proposed to retrieve data from the data management system GFHC used to track services for their clients. Here again we needed to balance the program and evaluation needs. As evaluators, we needed a tracking system to monitor how many calls AFRICAN received, the demographics of the clients, the needs of the clients, and the number and locations of client referrals. To protect client confidentiality, we needed to access the data without seeing clients' names. To minimize the burden on staff, we wanted open access to the collected data, so AFRICAN staff would not need to prepare reports for us.

GFHC required a system that could be accessed by both the centralized and decentralized navigators who would be working out of multiple offices at the same time. They needed to be able to access client data about individual problems and situations for their clients and be able to access what service providers were given referrals. To be able to provide the most appropriate referrals, AFRICAN staff needed to be able to ask and record screening questions, like race, employment, or zip code. Several local service providers had funds set aside for specific focus areas that were designated to be used by members of a particular race, the working poor, or residents living in specific locations.

Balancing Program and Evaluation Needs. We had several meetings with AFRICAN program staff about what type of data system could accomplish both program and evaluation needs. The system needed to be (A) Internet-based to allow decentralized navigators to access information, (B) Health

Insurance Portability and Accountability Act (HIPAA) compliant because clients would be providing protected health information (OPM, 2000), and (C) secure with appropriate firewalls to protect client confidentiality. The evaluators and GFHC staff researched several options and jointly created a "must" list so we could begin shopping for an Internet service provider.

Hurry Up and Wait. The search for an Internet service provider was time-consuming. GFHC was committed to using local resources when possible and made additional efforts when conducting community-based projects to secure vendors from within the community. Though we located a full-service data entry/program management system in Genesee County, this vendor was ultimately unable to write the code; address HIPAA and confidentiality concerns; and procure secure, dedicated servers, encryption software, and firewalls. Thus, the online data collection system was not in place when AFRICAN began taking calls in August 2005. As a result, GFHC created a paper form for recording information about each client and services provided. They entered data from the paper form into a spreadsheet document. Four months later, a company specializing in Web-based data management systems for social service providers was identified. Within a month of hiring the data management company, the new online system was up and running. However, the new system was not ideal for retrieving data for the evaluation study because the limited download capacity (8 to 10 variables each time) forced us to conduct multiple downloads and several data set matching and merging procedures. In addition, the Web page was "down" at times because of hardware problems.

Putting the Burden Back On. The paperwork created by AFRICAN staff during the time lag increased the burden for them and for the evaluation team. A member of the AFRICAN staff had to enter all of the previously collected information into the new system, and this cost the GFHC staff time. In addition, the data outputs available from the newly implemented system were cumbersome, and there were several limitations to the amount of data allowable for download. To complete complex analyses, the evaluation team had to merge several downloads into one database. The work was not especially hard or complicated, but it added costs to the project.

Putting Together the Wish List (Part II)

To assess client satisfaction with AFRICAN, we needed to talk directly to women who had contacted AFRICAN and had been referred to service providers. This meant creating a second data collection system. We needed to be able to contact clients, but we needed GFHC and the CBO navigators to obtain a "consent to contact" from the AFRICAN clients during their first call. A consent to contact question was added to the AFRICAN client intake protocol and included in the Web-based data management system. Once we had the names of clients who were willing to be contacted, the research team conducted further screening before making calls. Because the focus of this new program was to reduce infant mortality, we selected clients from the database who met the screening criteria (i.e., indicated they were pregnant women or parents/caregivers of a child under 2 years old).

LESSONS LEARNED

We learned a number of valuable lessons while conducting this evaluation study—mostly about how to be useful to a project that is just getting started when the evaluators were asked to play a dual role in terms of assisting in the development of both the project itself and the evaluation plans.

Being Open About Potential Role Conflicts

When the coordinating agency (GFHC) asked the lead evaluator to play a dual role, we were concerned about potential conflicts of interest. How could we serve both as a voting member of the committee guiding the program's development and as the hired evaluator of the same program? It was very helpful to take the time in critical planning meetings to explain our ideas and values about the appropriate role an evaluator should play in this type of program and how those values could be diminished if role conflicts arose. The sponsors and other partners indicated they understood the potential conflicts of interest, but they still endorsed the idea of the evaluator playing a dual role. To their credit, the evaluation reports we produced did not elicit the conflicts we anticipated. This may have been due to the care the lead evaluator took in monitoring his role in decision making related to the program's development.

Importance of Engaging Stakeholders

Incorporating the stakeholders into the program planning process and the evaluation design proved fruitful. People who live in and are a part of the community are valuable resources. By discussing the evaluation design and the research questions with the AFRICAN committees, we built consensus with the stakeholders. Community-based research/evaluation helps increase stakeholder ownership and commitment to the evaluation by focusing on results that are meaningful and culturally relevant to the stakeholders. The process of incorporating and fostering continuing engagement with stakeholders can be cumbersome and time-consuming, but the efforts pay off through stakeholders' increased commitment, which could increase the validity of the evaluation by ensuring community participation. Evaluators of community-based projects would be wise to revisit the old adage, "You need to give to get."

Revisiting Goals

Once we had generated the list of research questions, we strongly benefited by revisiting the overall goals of the program and the evaluation. For the duration of the program, we met monthly with the Operations Committee. We worked together to hone the evaluation's goals and objectives. If we had not revisited our goals, we might have wasted time and resources answering questions such as "What is the most effective way of social marketing the program?" which would have required a different methodology. If we had pursued this research question, we might have sacrificed needed funds on a research question that did not fall into our broad evaluation objectives. The group was able to posit some theories on the effectiveness of different social marketing techniques by correlating the type of advertising used (e.g., radio, television) and the number of calls in a given month.

Creative Solutions and Partnerships

By involving stakeholders in the evaluation planning, we were able to conceptualize a Web-based data management system that could meet the call center's needs and the evaluation needs. This "two-for-one" system for program tracking and evaluation provided a workable solution. The only problem that we experienced with the Web-based system was the system's limitations in downloading more than 10 variables, which forced us to conduct multiple data downloads and to match and merge data sets. We learned the importance of all players coming together at the planning stage. If we had not worked together and generated our program and evaluation data wish lists, we could have duplicated our efforts, increasing costs and possibly decreasing the evaluation's efficacy.

Flexibility or You Can't Always Think of Everything

To achieve the evaluation's goals, we needed to be flexible and willing to adapt the protocol to achieve results. Our new mantra is *leave yourself open to modifications*. After we conducted 30 interviews, we wrote a preliminary report on the results. After reviewing the report with the AFRICAN staff and committees, we realized that in our initial interview protocol we had asked the clients about their satisfaction with the AFRICAN program and which referral sources they had contacted, but we did not ask if the referral source had met their needs. To fully assess one of the three original research questions—How well did the program address the relevant issues of the program clients?—we needed to know about the clients' interactions with the community-based groups and health and human services organizations to which AFRICAN had referred them. To evaluate this interaction, we added a section to the interview that asked the clients the name of the organization that AFRICAN referred them to and whether they contacted the organization. We asked them to rate the organization on timeliness, friendliness, and ability to meet their needs. This helped us achieve the original evaluation goals by investigating if the referred service providers were actually helping the clients.

Our adaptability was essential even after we modified and adopted the interview. The goal of the AFRICAN project was to help women better access services already present in the community. Many of the clients required multiple referrals and had stressful life and financial situations. We found that the amount of financial (and perhaps emotional) stress in program participants' lives could take a toll on the evaluation study. When we designed the interview portion of the evaluation, we wanted to complete 150 interviews. Once we had established our list of willing and eligible clients and began to contact them, we found that many of the clients had moved or had interrupted phone service. We knew that the population was likely to be mobile and had tried to account for that fact. AFRICAN staff asked the clients for an additional contact phone number at the time of the initial call. Some clients did not have family or friends with working phones, or the phone numbers the clients provided as additional contacts were later disconnected.

Overall, it was difficult to contact many clients who were willing to participate in the interview. Of the 470 eligible women who had agreed to be contacted by the evaluators for further information on the study, we could complete interviews with only 106 clients (23% response rate). We missed our original goal of 150 interviews (31% response rate). In the planning stage, we should have considered the clients' life circumstances and reasons for calling AFRICAN. We should have considered that many AFRICAN clients were looking for financial help (e.g., help with heating bills, tangible goods, or medical assistance) and might have problems maintaining phone service. They may also change home addresses because of financial problems. To accommodate these possibilities, we should have asked AFRICAN navigators to provide the clients' mailing address in addition to their phone numbers, and we should have requested additional contact information (e.g., for a close friend or family member) when we first contacted the clients.

Another unplanned evaluation issue where flexibility was paramount to reaching goals was the inability of many clients to complete the interviews during "normal" work hours. Many clients worked during the day, and many more used cellular phones as their primary telephone. The interviewer had to accommodate the clients by calling them on weekends and evenings when the phones had "free minutes." About 40% of the interviews were conducted after hours and on weekends. Our staff needed to be able to accommodate the clients and speak with clients when it was convenient for them. If we had not been flexible and altered the call hours, we would have completed far fewer interviews.

Identify Contingency Plans

One of the easiest ways to stall an evaluation is to get locked into one mind-set, product, or vendor. We had successfully used the participatory process to blend AFRICAN's need for real-time access to data from multiple places with our desire to have data readily accessible to the evaluators for periodic evaluation reports. Conceiving the idea and developing a workable plan and system specifications took a lot of time, as did trying to use a local vendor to create the system. We wanted to use a local vendor because including community members in the project is another way for the community to benefit from the research. The concept of using local vendors from within the community of concern provides economic empowerment for the community (jobs and resources) (Springett, 2003). When working on a community-based project, it is prudent to use local vendors and hire individuals who represent the community of concern. We attempted to purchase programming and Internet access from local businesses that a member of the Operations Committee highly recommended. After months of detailing our wants and needs and working with the vendor to design a system, the vendor became nonresponsive, and we realized the vendor could not deliver the promised system within the needed time frame. We had to start the process anew.

Not having a computer system in place increased the burden on the program, AFRICAN staff, and the evaluators. Because we started the program with a paper system, the evaluation team could not produce timely periodic reports without the AFRICAN staff entering the data from paper forms into the online database. Once the new system was working, it took months for all of the calls recorded on paper to be entered into the Internet computer system. This time lag slowed the flow of data from the evaluators to the program staff, making it difficult to assess progress. Without current data, the planning committees had to make some assumptions about staffing and marketing.

Reflecting back on this problem, we knew that the Web-based data management system was necessary for the evaluation study, and we should have encouraged GFHC to search for vendors outside as well as within the Flint/Genesee County community. If we had had a contingency plan in place, we may have saved time and labor for both the program and evaluation staff.

Transferring Lessons to Other Evaluation Projects

The lessons we learned in developing and executing an evaluation plan for this project were specific to this project and transcended this project. Evaluators must consider levels of context (e.g., local versus global), levels of abstraction (e.g., grounded versus conceptual), and levels of relationships (e.g., interpersonal versus political) in almost every evaluation project. In designing an evaluation project, one must consider important analytical issues such as theories of causality in research methodologies, as well as practical matters such as costs and participation burden.

We learned from this project and others like it that to be useful, evaluation researchers need to respond to the needs of the various stakeholders involved. That is a general lesson, but there can be no set of directions for how to do this. To borrow from an old political adage: all evaluations are local. The evaluator must be responsive to local needs but must also provide a general way of thinking about research methods and general research competencies that can be applied to local circumstances. We believe that the lessons we learned will be valuable as we conduct other evaluation studies, but only if they are applied to the specific circumstances of those new projects.

CONCLUSION

Final Evaluation Design

The final evaluation design involved two data collection efforts. The first data collection effort focused on describing the program's implementation by tracking the number of new clients served by the project and describing the clients who accessed the project's services. We used the client tracking system to create summaries from the AFRICAN client database. This database recorded important background information about every individual who called the AFRICAN information and referral service and about individuals who had been in face-to-face contact with one of the AFRICAN navigators and had agreed to have their information recorded in the AFRICAN database for future reference.

The database recorded clients' demographics, including gender, race, age, number of children, pregnancy status, and employment. From this information, we could determine the number of clients per month, the demographics of the average client, and whether the AFRICAN clients were representative of the community of concern. We also recorded each client's request for assistance and the referrals given to each client. From this information, we could provide the committees with periodic reports on frequencies of the type of need reported by the clients. We reported the counts and percentages of the service providers to which the clients were referred. The committees could use this information as a form of process evaluation to monitor the number of calls and the client demographics. The same information was useful for the impact evaluation. At the end of the program, we could identify the number of people affected by the intervention, the number of referrals provided, and the identities of the referred service providers.

The second data collection effort was an interview study that the evaluation team conducted with AFRICAN clients a few weeks after they received information and referral services. AFRICAN staff members made the initial contact with potential respondents either over the telephone or in face-to-face visits in clinics and service settings. Near the end of these service or outreach interactions, the AFRICAN staff member asked the potential respondent if they would be interested in participating in an evaluation study of AFRICAN's services. The potential respondent was told that participants would receive a $25 gift card. Participants who agreed to be interviewed and met the screening criteria (i.e., had been pregnant in the past 12 months or pregnant at the time of the screening, or were the parent or caregiver of a child aged 2 years or younger) were interviewed after completing a signed consent form. This information was stored in the AFRICAN program database and made available to the evaluation study staff.

With this information, we could provide the committees with periodic reports providing the level of satisfaction with AFRICAN and the service providers referred by AFRICAN. We reported the means of ratings and information about the client's relationship with pediatric and prenatal medical providers. The committees could use this information as a form of process evaluation, ensuring the quality of service provided by AFRICAN.

Compromises

Evaluation methods can be very powerful ways to examine the implementation and effects of a program. Nevertheless, every method is limited in some way; for example, evaluators may choose the wrong measures, the comparisons (between groups or within groups) may be invalid, or the data may be misinterpreted. Evaluation researchers are ethically obligated to share what they know (or suspect) about the methodological flaws in their designs. In this evaluation study, we were able to help build a client data information system with carefully designed questions and responses to help us describe the clients who received services. But our data were only as good as the diligence of the project staff and the reliability of their response choices and data entry (which was never assessed). We also could develop an interview protocol that allowed us to ask clients about the quality of the project and other health services they received. We used comparison data from similar populations collected 2 years earlier. Our conclusions about the clients' experiences, however, must be tempered because the sample that accessed the AFRICAN services was not randomly drawn from the same population assessed in the earlier study.

Call and Response

The development of the evaluation plan was responsive to the information needs of the project's sponsors and other key stakeholders and was responsive to the creation of the new community-based program. This process took about a year to unfold. Our ideas for developing a usable, feasible, ethical, and accurate evaluation plan evolved as we learned more about the development of the program. This amount of time also enabled all the key stakeholders to hear our evaluation plan proposals and provide feedback to our planning processes. This improvisational process required trust and patience even under pressure to implement as soon as possible. But in the end, we believe our ability to be responsive and flexible and the patience demonstrated by all key stakeholders allowed us to successfully respond to the program's call.

NOTE

1. Friendly Access[SM] was a national demonstration project conceived and developed by the Lawton and Rhea Chiles Center for Healthy Mothers and Babies at the University of South Florida School of Public Health and implemented in four communities including Flint/Genesee County, Michigan (see http://www.chilescenter .org/programs4.htm).

REFERENCES

Brandon, D. T., Isaac, L. A., & LaVeist, T. A. (2005). The legacy of Tuskegee and trust in medical care: Is Tuskegee responsible for race differences in mistrust of medical care? *Journal of the National Medical Association, 97*(7), 951–956.

Centers for Disease Control and Prevention. (2007). *Racial and ethnic approaches to community health.* Retrieved October 15, 2007, from http://www.cdc.gov/reach/

Cook, C. A., Selig, K. L., Wedge, B. J., & Gohn-Baube, E. A. (1999). Access barriers and the use of prenatal care by low income, inner-city women. *Social Work, 44*(2), 129–139.

Greater Flint Health Coalition. (2005). *About us.* Retrieved May 6, 2008, from http://www.gfhc.org/a-background.html

Joint Committee on Standards for Educational Evaluation. (1994). *The program evaluation standards: How to assess evaluations of educational programs* (2nd ed.). Thousand Oaks, CA: Sage.

Michigan Department of Community Health. (2007). *2002–2006 Michigan resident birth and death files. Vital records & health data development section.* Retrieved October 15, 2007, from http://www.mdch.state.mi.us/PhA/OSR/ index.asp?Id=3

Office of Personnel Management. (2000). *HIPPA Consumer Bill of Rights and Responsibilities.* Retrieved December 10, 2007, from http://www.opm.gov/ insure/health/cbrr.htm

Schulz, A. J., Israel, B. A., Selig, S. M., Bayer, I. S., & Griffin, C. B. (1998). Development and implementation of principles for community-based research in public health. In R. H. MacNair (Ed.), *Research strategies for community practice* (pp. 83–110). New York: Haworth Press.

Smitherman, G. (1977). *Talkin and testifyin: The language of black America.* Detroit: Wayne State University Press.

Springett, J. (2003). Issues in participatory evaluation. In M. Minkler & N. Wallerstein (Eds.), *Community-based participatory research for health* (pp. 263–288). San Francisco: Jossey-Bass.

Stake, R. E. (2004a). Stake and responsive evaluation. In M. C. Alkin (Ed.), *Evaluation roots: Tracing theorists' views and influences* (pp. 203–217). Thousand Oaks, CA: Sage.

Stake, R. E. (2004b). *Standards-based and responsive evaluation.* Thousand Oaks, CA: Sage.

Stufflebeam, D. L. (2001). Evaluation models. *New Directions for Evaluation, 89,* 7–98.

Stufflebeam, D. L., & Shinkfield, A. J. (2007). *Evaluation theory, models, and applications.* San Francisco: Jossey-Bass.

U.S. Department of Health and Human Services, Health Resources and Services Administration, Maternal and Child Health Bureau. (2004). *Child health USA 2004.* Rockville, MD: U.S. Author.

6

PLANNING FOR A
MEDIA EVALUATION

W. Douglas Evans, Kevin C. Davis,
and Matthew C. Farrelly

Media evaluation is an overarching subject area that includes the study of marketing campaigns intended to promote or change consumer behavior, as well as assessments of educational and entertainment media and the effects of news media on public discourse and policy. In this chapter, we focus on the evaluation of health communication and marketing campaigns designed to affect consumer health behavior. In this domain, media evaluation is distinct from other forms of program evaluation in that it focuses specifically on behavior change through marketing and promotion of healthy behaviors or avoidance of unhealthy behaviors, as opposed to broad evaluation strategies that cross-cut multiple venues and approaches. After providing some background on health communication and marketing, we describe the evaluation of the truth® countermarketing campaign, the largest antitobacco media campaign conducted in the United States to date.

HEALTH COMMUNICATION AND MARKETING

Health communication "encompasses the study and use of communication strategies to inform and influence individual and community decisions that enhance health" (Freimuth, Cole, & Kirby, 2001, p. 475). *Healthy People 2010* (*HP2010*) categorizes health communication as a national public health priority because of its pervasive role throughout all aspects of health. For example, the majority of the leading health indicators identified in *HP2010* (e.g., regular physical activity, healthy weight, tobacco use, access to health care, risk communication, emergent health threats) are dependent on effective health communication (U.S. Department of Health and Human Services, 2000).

Social marketing is a form of health communication that seeks to influence social behaviors, not to benefit the marketer but to benefit the target audience and society as a whole (Kotler & Zaltman, 1971). Social marketing attempts to increase healthy behaviors in a population by using some of the proven marketing techniques used to promote commercial products (Kotler & Andreasen, 1996). These techniques mirror those in commercial marketing and are based on the marketing mix, or 4 Ps of marketing: place, price, product, and promotion (Borden, 1964). Recently, the combined fields of health communication and social marketing have been referred to simply as "health communication and marketing" (Evans, 2006).

Mass media is one of the main channels by which health communication and marketing messages are communicated to audiences. Media campaigns, and the methods and design of media evaluations, are based on social marketing theory and behavioral theory, including theories of exposure, messaging, communication, and behavior change (Hornik, 2002).

MEDIA EVALUATION

Media evaluation is an important source of information on the development, implementation, and effectiveness of social marketing initiatives, and the truth® campaign is a major recent example. As discussed later in this chapter, truth® is a branded, national tobacco-use prevention media campaign designed to reach adolescents, ages 12 to 17, primarily through edgy television advertisements with an anti–tobacco industry theme (Farrelly et al., 2002; Farrelly, Davis, Haviland, Messeri, & Healton, 2005). Young adults, ages 18 to 24, comprise an important secondary audience. The campaign launched in 2000 and is the only national youth smoking prevention campaign in the United States not sponsored by the tobacco industry.

Media evaluation can be divided into process and outcome evaluation methods (Evans & Hastings, 2008). Process evaluation helps to assess whether (1) the target audience has been exposed to a campaign's messages (e.g., did adolescents hear the truth® campaign message?) and (2) the target audience reacts favorably to the messages in real-world circumstances (e.g., how did adolescents react to truth® messages when they heard them?). Outcome evaluation helps to determine the effects of messages on health behavior and determinants of behavior, such as health knowledge, attitudes, and beliefs (e.g., were adolescents who heard truth® messages less likely to try smoking or become an established smoker?).

Media evaluations often capture process and outcome data simultaneously to offer the immediate formative feedback that can enhance the campaign effort (Evans & Hastings, 2008). At the same time, immediate reactions to media messages and outcomes are correlated, and thus process and outcome evaluation efforts need to work hand in hand. The following example of the truth® campaign illustrates how media evaluations are based on measuring four key process and outcome dimensions of campaign effectiveness:

• Exposure and recall
• Message reactions and receptivity
• Behavioral determinants (knowledge, attitudes, and beliefs)
• Behavioral outcomes

BACKGROUND ON THE truth® CAMPAIGN MEDIA EVALUATION PROJECT

In February 2000, the American Legacy Foundation (Legacy) launched the national truth® tobacco countermarketing campaign, the largest social marketing effort to prevent and control youth smoking ever undertaken in the United States. In its first year, truth® had a budget of more than $100 million and aired tobacco prevention advertising spots in major metropolitan demographic market areas (DMAs) across the country.

The truth® campaign was based on the Florida TRUTH campaign, which reduced rates of youth tobacco use in Florida (Bauer, Johnson, Hopkins, & Brooks, 2000). The intellectual roots of both the Florida TRUTH campaign (which ended in 2004 due to lack of funding) and Legacy's national truth® campaign are in the work of a panel of youth marketing experts convened in 1996 by the Columbia School of Public Health and funded by the Centers for Disease Control and Prevention (CDC) (Columbia Marketing Panel, 1996; McKenna, Gutierrez, & McCall, 2000). The Columbia panel identified three critical elements for a successful youth tobacco prevention media campaign. First, noting adolescents' extreme brand consciousness and the pervasiveness of tobacco brands, the panel called for the creation of a teen-focused nonsmoking, or "countermarketing," brand. Second, it recognized that a teen-focused campaign must talk to adolescents in their own voice rather than talking down to them. Third, the panel recommended that the countermarketing brand highlight the actions of the tobacco industry in marketing cigarettes, including its failures to be truthful about cigarettes' addictiveness and health effects (Columbia Marketing Panel, 1996; McKenna,

Gutierrez, & McCall, 2000). These became key elements of Legacy's national truth® campaign.

The primary objectives of the truth® campaign were to (1) expose youth to truth® messages and promote positive reactions to those messages, (2) change attitudes and beliefs toward tobacco use and the tobacco industry, and (3) reduce tobacco use among youth. These three objectives formed the road map for an evaluation plan that first aimed to develop measures of youth exposure to the campaign; then to assess the relationship between campaign exposure and related knowledge, attitudes, and beliefs; and finally to assess whether the campaign was associated with reduced youth smoking prevalence.

Though the campaign's objectives suggest a fairly straightforward road map for evaluation planning, the implementation of this evaluation was complex due to a number of contextual factors, including the relationship between the evaluators and the advertisers and marketers who designed and implemented the campaign, evaluation design and measurement challenges, and environmental factors external to the campaign (including trends in tobacco use). Each of these factors presented challenges to isolating and assessing the effects of the truth® campaign on tobacco-related outcomes among youth.

The goal of the truth® campaign evaluation plan was to conceive and design a series of studies that would simultaneously account for these factors while being sensitive enough to detect campaign effects. Below we describe the primary elements of evaluation design and execution intended to address these three objectives with emphasis on how the evaluation plan was shaped by specific challenges.

ASSESS CONTEXT

A number of important differences exist between the context of media evaluation and other forms of evaluation planning. The primary difference is that assessment of the population and media context is primarily the province of the media campaign developers. Media evaluators are not responsible for—and typically have limited involvement in—identifying the target audience, developing messages, and choosing media channels through which to deliver a media campaign. For the truth® campaign evaluation, assessing the context for truth® consisted mainly of determining how media evaluation measurement and evaluation design strategies could best be tailored to the three major truth® campaign objectives.

Measure Exposure and Message Reactions

The first objective of the truth® campaign was to increase youth exposure to truth® messages and generate positive audience receptivity to those messages. Because truth® was implemented with a fluid media schedule with new ads and subcampaigns (i.e., distinct messages that related to and supported the larger truth® messages) appearing regularly, a continuous media tracking survey of youth in the United States was needed to capture awareness of and reactions to the campaign and receptivity to its messages. At the time of the campaign's launch in 2000, telephone surveys could be administered quickly and relatively inexpensively while providing a nationally representative picture of youth awareness of the campaign. Because truth® also targeted specific racial and ethnic groups, a telephone Legacy Media Tracking Survey (LMTS) was designed to provide estimates of campaign awareness and receptivity among 12- to 17-year-olds overall and separately among African American and Hispanic youth.

Awareness of the campaign was measured using a variety of metrics. Simple recall of truth® would not be sufficient for identifying how many youth were exposed to specific messages. Thus, the LMTS included specific measures of confirmed awareness of each truth® ad that was airing at any given time. These measures required respondents to identify specific features of the ads to confirm that they had actually seen them. The LMTS also included other, more general measures such as a construct that captured overall awareness of the truth® campaign brand.

It was also important to assess how youth reacted to truth® campaign messages. Did youth who saw campaign messages react to those messages favorably? To examine this, the truth® campaign's evaluation plan called for measurement of a number of ad receptivity constructs, which captured the degree to which youth responded favorably or unfavorably to specific messages. These measures included whether an ad was "believable" or "gave good reasons not to smoke." The inclusion of these types of measures in the evaluation was based on the Elaboration Likelihood Model (ELM), which asserts that attitudinal changes are a function of the level of cognitive elaboration and information-processing activity that occurs regarding a particular message (Petty & Cacioppo, 1986).

From a practical standpoint, continuous tracking of campaign awareness and receptivity to campaign messages provided real-time feedback to the campaign's media contractors, creative directors, and other stakeholders involved in designing and implementing truth® ads. Specifically, continuous tracking provided the campaign's implementation team with useful information on whether the campaign was reaching its youth audience and whether course corrections in message content were needed. The evaluation plan included strategies for sharing these data with the campaign's media contractors on a regular basis. Another, perhaps more important, function of these measures was to facilitate an examination of the relationship between exposure to the campaign and cognitive precursors to smoking. Therefore, the LMTS also included a wide range of items that measured specific knowledge, attitudes, and beliefs that were central to truth®'s messages and believed to be predictors of the likelihood of smoking initiation. The novelty of the campaign's messages presented challenges for identifying these measures and necessitated an evaluation planning process that was closely integrated with the campaign's creative development.

Assess Attitudinal Changes

Unlike many youth campaigns before it, the truth® campaign was marketed as a brand, similar to other youth brands, to appeal to adolescents most at risk of smoking. At the time of the truth® campaign's launch, the use of "branded" health messages that marketed the benefits of buying into a brand like truth® was relatively new. Aside from several measures used in evaluations of the Florida TRUTH campaign, there were few specific measures of knowledge, attitudes, and beliefs related to these sorts of messages. Thus, new measures had to be conceptualized that not only captured the essence of truth® messages but were also associated with the likelihood of smoking initiation.

The initial wave of the LMTS was fielded in December 1999, prior to the launch of the truth® campaign, to determine baseline levels of tobacco-related knowledge, attitudes, and beliefs. Before the baseline LMTS was fielded, campaign evaluators participated in intensive meetings with media contractor staff to learn about the specific content of truth® messages and then develop measures of knowledge, attitudes, and beliefs that would be influenced by the specific message content. A second wave of the LMTS was conducted 10 months after the launch of the campaign. The first evaluation study published on these data showed that the campaign had made significant progress in achieving its first two goals. Awareness of the campaign was high, as approximately 75% of 12- to 17-year-olds in the United States reported being exposed to specific ads. There were also significant changes in knowledge, attitudes, and beliefs related to truth® messages 10 months after the launch of the campaign, and these changes were statistically associated with exposure to the campaign (Farrelly et al., 2002).

The LMTS continued to be the primary tool for evaluating awareness of and reactions to the truth® campaign during its first 3 years (2000 to 2003). During this time, the LMTS continued to evolve as the campaign frequently introduced new ads and subcampaigns. Thus, the evaluation planning process was iterative and ongoing in assessing campaign context and in identifying and developing needed attitudinal and behavioral measures. This process included continued and regular meetings with the campaign's creative directors and media contractors to determine what the new campaign messages and concepts were going to be and thus what types of attitudes and beliefs to measure in the LMTS. This process was also necessary for the more fundamental task of determining what specific ads were going to air over a given period and thus which ads should be asked about in the LMTS instrument.

Assess Behavioral Impact

With its flexibility to be implemented multiple times a year and its ability to provide timely and continuous data on campaign awareness, receptivity, and campaign-related knowledge, attitudes, and beliefs, the LMTS was ideal for examining the first two objectives of the truth® campaign. However, accurately measuring youth tobacco use via telephone surveys is challenging. Youth who are smokers, or have recently experimented with tobacco, are often reluctant to provide truthful responses when their parents are present in the home, which results in significant underreporting of smoking among youth in telephone surveys. Thus, the third overall objective of the truth® campaign, reducing youth tobacco use, needed to be assessed with a more suitable method: in-school surveys. In-school surveys such as the National Youth Tobacco Survey (NYTS) and Monitoring the Future (MTF) are more appropriate for measuring substance use because they are self-administered without the presence of parents or others who could motivate youth to provide socially desirable responses to substance use questions. With its large national sample and coverage of major media markets where the truth® campaign was advertised, MTF became the cornerstone of evaluation planning efforts to assess the campaign's impact on youth smoking behaviors. However, the specific design of this component of the evaluation was influenced by a number of challenges stemming from the implementation of the campaign's media strategy.

The most significant factor that influenced evaluation planning of behavioral changes was the fact that Legacy decided to implement the truth® campaign nationally with no control or comparison markets. All television markets in the United States received at least some exposure to the truth® campaign. This decision was based on a number of considerations, including the prior success of the Florida TRUTH campaign. First, given the dramatic success demonstrated in Florida, it would not be ethical to withhold the truth® campaign in any of the U.S. television markets. A second, practical consideration was that nationally aired advertising campaigns are more cost-efficient than spot purchases on a market-by-market basis.

This implementation strategy presented a fundamental challenge to evaluating the campaign's effects on smoking behaviors. Specifically, the lack of a control or comparison group (i.e., a group that was not exposed to the truth® campaign) presented a fundamental challenge to evaluating the campaign's effects on smoking behaviors. However, the variation in level of exposure from market to market created natural quasi-experimental comparison groups across the country.

Variation in the level of exposure by market was primarily due to the market-level availability of television stations on which truth® commercials were aired. During the launch of the campaign and into the first 2 years of implementation, Legacy's media strategy was to use national media buys dominated by advertising on broadcast network and syndicated television stations. This strategy produced a natural pattern of high variability in market-to-market delivery of the campaign. This variability in exposure stemmed from the fact that some networks on which the truth® campaign advertised (e.g., UPN, WB) were not available in certain markets, thereby creating a wide range of exposure levels across the country. These natural quasi-experimental comparison groups across the country provided a basis for examining associations between the "dose" of truth® campaign advertising at the market level and youth smoking prevalence.

The evaluation plan for assessing the behavioral impact of the truth® campaign thus called for multivariable analyses that made use of the natural variation in exposure across markets over time to isolate the impact of the truth® campaign on youth smoking behavior. This was achieved by obtaining market-level cumulative gross rating points (GRPs) for truth® from the campaign's media contractor. These data were linked to individual-level data on adolescents in the MTF surveys and were used to estimate the association between market-level exposure to the truth® campaign and youth smoking prevalence.

Another important consideration in the evaluation planning process for the truth® campaign was environmental context. At the time of the campaign's launch, there were many other factors that could have affected youth smoking prevalence apart from any effects of the truth® campaign.

For example, many states were building their own media campaigns and other interventions with funds from the 1998 Master Settlement Agreement. State-level investments in tobacco control programs were also increasing, as were cigarette prices and taxes, and these factors are also linked to youth smoking prevalence. At the same time, the tobacco industry was mounting national youth prevention campaigns of its own, including the Philip Morris "Think. Don't Smoke" campaign. Unless the truth® evaluation accounted for all of these factors, critics could argue that declines in youth smoking would have happened in the absence of the campaign and that those declines could be attributed to these external factors.

One of the most important aspects of early truth® evaluation planning was to ensure that the evaluation accounted for as many external influences on smoking as possible so that the effects of the truth® campaign could be readily isolated. Thus, by design, the truth® evaluation studies were well controlled. Two seminal evaluation studies for the truth® campaign (Farrelly et al., 2002; Farrelly et al., 2005) used state-level data on inflation-adjusted cigarette prices and investments in tobacco control program funding to control for other interventions that were happening apart from truth®. Studies that relied on the LMTS also tracked confirmed awareness of other campaigns including the industry-sponsored "Think. Don't Smoke" campaign and a number of state campaigns. These types of influences were found to be important correlates of youth smoking. Thus, controlling for external interventions and policies that could confound the effects of the truth® campaign enhanced the evaluation's ability to identify and isolate the effects of the campaign on smoking-related outcomes.

GATHER RECONNAISSANCE

As noted previously, one important difference between media evaluation and other areas of evaluation is direct interaction with the audience and setting in which the program and evaluation will occur. Media evaluators are typically one step removed from the target audience that will receive campaign messages and interact directly with media campaign developers. Thus, in this context, it is important to understand the strategy being used by campaign developers and use evaluation measures and methods that are sensitive to the campaign strategy.

In a series of in-person interviews conducted by evaluators in 2000, the designers and developers of the truth® campaign—advertising executives with a consortium of media contractors—articulated the basic strategy behind its advertising: build a teen-oriented brand to compete head-to-head with tobacco industry brands like the Marlboro man, Joe Camel, and the No Bull campaign (Evans, Wasserman, Bertolotti, & Martino, 2002). The advertisers reported that truth® would build a brand similar to other brands that appeal to adolescents, such as Nike, Converse, and Mountain Dew, rather than communicate a public health and education message about health risks or other reasons not to start smoking. Branding was seen as a key strategy to meet Legacy's goal of reducing smoking prevalence by removing its appeal and thereby changing social norms about smoking. Branding in this case required the establishment of idealized social images to which the audience (primarily adolescents) would aspire. Motivating young people to aspire to the image embodied in the brand was perceived as the best way to reach adolescents and essential to competing with the idealized social images created by the tobacco industry. The basic idea was to use challenging, thought-provoking ad contexts and images of adolescents in control, rebelling against forces that would prevent them from expressing their independence (i.e., the tobacco industry). Eye-catching creative material would allow the campaign to adapt quickly and provide the audience with new images to keep the brand fresh and alive (Evans et al., 2002).

From its inception, the truth® brand had several distinctive characteristics. First, a high level of adolescent influence over the brand was deemed critical. In the campaign's first months of development and immediately after its launch in February 2000, adolescents played a central role in planning as well as message design and development. They were viewed as controlling the brand and the methods used to deliver the message (e.g., advertising, events, gear). As truth® was initially conceived, its creators felt that adolescents had to control the message because they knew brands and readily identified with them. Through their leadership, the brand would seem real, fresh, and guaranteed to satisfy adolescents' most important need states: control, independence, and rebellion.

A second distinctive characteristic of the truth® brand strategy was the individuals' sense of being part of a social movement. Campaign designers intended that truth® would become a movement toward which adolescents would feel a sense of commitment and even ownership. Part of the brand identity was based on fostering the feeling that an adolescent who was slightly out of the mainstream and not prone to joining established groups (e.g., student council, sports teams) might be interested in being part of a group with an outside-the-mainstream mission. Much like the early Vietnam antiwar protesters, truth® adolescents would take up the mantle against the establishment (in this case, the tobacco industry) and create an environment that fostered camaraderie and a sense of mission (Evans et al., 2002).

Third, the concept of "vaccinating" youth against tobacco was another distinctive characteristic of the truth® brand. The idea was to create protective factors to counter the attributes of open-to-smoking adolescents that expose them to the risk of smoking. If these young people could develop a sense of control over their lives through brand affiliation and rebellion against the source of exposure to smoking and tobacco industry manipulation, they would have a clear-cut replacement for smoking: they would have a better brand (Evans, Price, & Blahut, 2005).

Most literature on industry manipulation campaigns (i.e., campaigns that focus on industry efforts to manipulate audience behavior to promote smoking) attributes their success to the fact that they tap into adolescents' natural tendency to rebel against authority figures and redirect it against the tobacco industry. Goldman and Glantz (1998) studied several different antismoking advertising strategies and suggested that industry manipulation campaigns reconfigured the parent–rebellious child dynamic by providing youth with a new enemy—the tobacco industry. Sly, Hopkins, Trapido, and Ray (2001) studied the attitudes of adolescents exposed to the Florida TRUTH campaign and proposed that "young people who receive [industry manipulation] messages develop negative attitudes toward the industry and the behavior it promotes, and in turn, make it more important for young people to not identify with the industry and the behavior it promotes" (p. 237).

Change as a result of exposure to truth® begins with awareness of truth® ads and the campaign as a whole, and it ends with the decision not to smoke. In between are a series of complex changes in youth attitudes, beliefs, and behaviors related to the tobacco industry; perceived health risks from smoking; social images of smoking; perceptions of smoking prevalence among peers; exposure to secondhand smoke; and so on. The evaluation challenge is to understand the continuum of change that occurs between being exposed to truth® and choosing not to smoke, and the relationships among variables on that continuum. As an initial step, evaluators must first understand the perceived value of the truth® brand to adolescents.

ENGAGE STAKEHOLDERS

Stakeholders for media evaluations differ in some important respects from stakeholders for other types of evaluations. Evaluation planning efforts for media evaluations typically involve a sponsor, at least one media contractor responsible for designing and executing the media campaign, and one or more evaluators as stakeholders. The members of the target audience, or population on behalf of which the media campaign is conducted, are critical stakeholders of the campaign but not of the evaluators per se. In the context of media campaigns, evaluators are one step removed from involvement with the audience in that consideration of audience attitudes, beliefs, preferences, media habits, and other factors relevant to developing effective messages will have been addressed by the sponsor and media contractor outside the evaluation context. The media contractor typically conducts formative research (e.g., interviews and focus groups to understand audience habits and opportunities for behavior change) and thus interacts directly with the audience, whereas the evaluator does not.

The same is true of other policymaking and community groups that may be interested in the campaign and the evaluation's findings. Clearly, they are stakeholders in the sense that they have an interest in the evaluation. However, the media campaign evaluator operates outside the context of these actors because the data are exposure to a campaign and a set of media executions of the campaign created and distributed by the media contractor on behalf of the sponsor. The evaluator does not interact with the target audience and other immediate participants in the evaluation as a stakeholder; the media contractor is an intermediary between the evaluator and the audience.

For example, the truth® campaign evaluators conducted a process evaluation of the campaign's design and development. This included interviews and observation of media contractor activities and resulted in articulation of the truth® brand strategy (Evans et al., 2002). Thus, the immediate stakeholders for the evaluation were the marketing executives, who relayed information to the evaluators about the target audience as stakeholders and how the campaign would attempt to reach them.

To stay in touch with the campaign as it developed over time, evaluators remained engaged with the media contractors as key stakeholders. After the initial process evaluation, evaluators regularly met with the campaign designers to learn about new advertisements and other activities. Evaluators also shared evaluation findings with the campaign designers and provided customized analyses to help with campaign planning. One example was evaluation data on truth® brand efforts, which were used to provide feedback to campaign designers on how audience reactions could be measured and how desired brand associations such as loyalty or perceptions of quality could be enhanced.

In turn, input from the campaign designers was used by evaluators to focus the evaluation. As described in the next section, this process continued for several years during the truth® evaluation.

FOCUS THE EVALUATION

Because the truth® campaign was planned for nationwide launch and designed to continue over an extended period, there was no opportunity for experimental design. Instead, evaluators developed the LMTS, which became the primary evaluation tool used in the campaign.

The LMTS captured data on all the key process and outcome data outlined above, including the following:

- Tobacco use behavior
  - Smoking frequency and quantity
  - Smokeless tobacco use
- Smoking-related knowledge, attitudes, and beliefs
- Campaign-related knowledge, attitudes, and beliefs
  - Attitudes toward tobacco industry
  - Beliefs about health effects of tobacco use
- truth® brand measures
  - Awareness of the brand
  - Associations with brand characteristics
  - Media habits and other message exposure
  - Television, radio, print, and Internet use
  - Exposure to other tobacco and antitobacco messages
- truth® campaign exposure
  - Awareness of specific advertisements
  - Reactions and receptivity to messages
- Sociodemographic characteristics

Development of the LMTS as a process and outcome evaluation tool was iterative. As noted earlier, the campaign developed over time, adding new subcampaigns, advertisements, and messages. At the time it was developed in late 1999, the LMTS consisted of core elements that were closely tied to what evaluators knew about the campaign plans, having gained insight into those plans by talking to campaign designers. Between 2000 and 2003, the LMTS was conducted nine times to measure population-level campaign awareness and outcomes, and during this time evaluators continued to work with campaign designers to develop new measures and eliminate some old ones.

Evaluators developed and removed items from the LTMS over time in three main ways:

1. A team of evaluators (called a survey improvement committee) reviewed information gathered from campaign designers and other sources, formulated evaluation questions, and developed relevant new survey items.
2. Evaluators reviewed new truth® campaign advertisements—television, radio, print—to determine specific advertisements, broad messages, and campaign-related attitudes to add to the survey.
3. Because the purpose of the evaluation was to monitor the campaign and evaluate changes in tobacco-related attitudes, beliefs, and behaviors, evaluators eliminated some items that were either no longer relevant to campaign activities or had reached their "ceiling" (i.e., they were no longer changing or likely to show any appreciable increase).

These techniques ensured that the LMTS evolved along with the campaign and remained a sensitive instrument.

The evaluation aimed to measure the effects of the national campaign on smoking behavior and its behavioral determinants. One of the main evaluation questions was "What is the dose-response effect of truth® exposure?" However, this presented a design challenge because there was no experimental control. The evaluators' solution was to use natural variation in exposure to the campaign across media markets as a market-specific measure of the dose of truth®. Dose by media market was then used as a control variable in analyses.

Environmental measures of brand exposure rely on DMA (media market) data such as GRPs to provide estimates of population exposure in specific media markets. Many mass media campaigns buy advertising based on media outlet availability (e.g., television stations widely viewed by the target audience) and media market characteristics (e.g., size, demographics, pricing). GRPs represent an estimate of viewership of paid media based on data derived from sources such as AC Nielsen. These data can be used to estimate population exposure to advertising aired during a given time on a particular station.

Environmental exposure data represent both a means of estimating campaign reach and a tool that evaluators can use to introduce natural variation in audience exposure. In turn, this can be used as an analytical tool, a kind of natural experimental control (Rossi & Freeman, 1993). Farrelly et al. (2005) used GRP data to estimate the effects of truth® on adolescent smoking over the first 3 years of the campaign. In the truth® evaluation, natural variation in media buying among media markets in a national campaign was used as a variable to account for differences in smoking behavior and changes in smoking over time in a population as a result of the level of exposure. Figure 6.1 summarizes the variation in truth® campaign exposure across the United States, with darker areas having higher scores on an exposure index based on GRPs of the truth® campaign delivered in those media markets. The launch of truth® coincided with the early stages of a period of declining adolescent smoking rates. Another challenge to evaluating truth® was to analytically account for the existence of an independent trend in youth smoking and to determine what proportion of that trend was attributable to the campaign. This was a major challenge in the analysis of campaign outcomes, given (1) the absence of control (non-truth®) DMAs without campaign exposure; (2) environmental conditions in which smoking rates were changing independent of the campaign; and (3) changes in the campaign media buying, advertisements, and other external factors varying independently over time.

However, the natural variation in truth® exposure across DMAs presented an opportunity to use campaign dose to control for these factors and identify

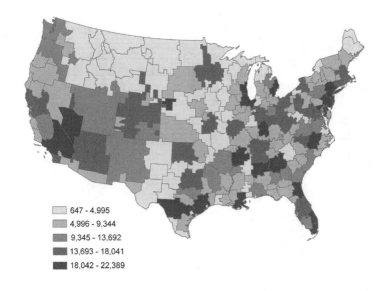

647 - 4,995
4,996 - 9,344
9,345 - 13,692
13,693 - 18,041
18,042 - 22,389

Figure 6.1   Variation in truth® Campaign GRPs by Media Markets (2000–2002)

SOURCE: From Farrelly, M. C., Davis, K. C., Haviland, M. Lyndon, Messeri, P., & Healton, C. G. (2005). Evidence of a Dose-Response Relationship Between 'Truth' Antismoking Ads and Youth Smoking Prevalence. *American Journal of Public Health*, 95(3), 425-431.

a dose-response effect. Farrelly et al. (2005) analyzed LMTS tracking data and national data on adolescent smoking rates and found that 22% of the total decline in youth smoking was attributable to the truth® campaign. Figure 6.2 compares the actual trend in youth smoking to the predicted trend in the absence of the truth® campaign.

The 22% effect of truth® on smoking is relatively large by social marketing standards (see Snyder & Hamilton, 2002, for a review of effect sizes in social marketing, which typically range from 5% to 9% for effective campaigns). The campaign's practical significance is perhaps even greater, as it represents roughly 300,000 fewer U.S. youth smokers over a 3-year period as a result of truth® (Farrelly et al., 2005).

LESSONS LEARNED

A number of important lessons learned from the truth® campaign evaluation illustrate the challenges in conducting a media evaluation and suggest

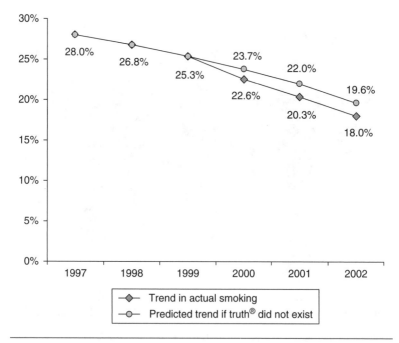

Figure 6.2   Portion of Decline in Adolescent Smoking Attributable to truth®

SOURCE: Adapted from Farrelly et al. (2005).

opportunities for future media evaluation planning. Overall, the truth® evaluation planning benefited from substantial financial resources and from being based on a previous, effective media campaign and evaluation effort: Florida TRUTH. However, challenges included the need for very rapid start-up, the lack of opportunity for experimental control, and the need to remain sensitive to an evolving campaign with multiple stakeholders (not all of which the evaluators had direct or regular access to).

Several specific lessons emerge from this chapter:

- The truth® campaign was one of the largest public health campaigns, and the media evaluation was one of the largest ever conducted.
- As such, it required multiple evaluation methods (process and outcome, different instruments and analysis techniques).
- A number of campaign-related decisions, like national launch, influenced evaluators' decisions about evaluation design, methods, and measures.
- More consideration of the impact of campaign decisions (especially early ones), and evaluator input into them, would benefit future media evaluations.
- Regular interaction with the media contractor was extremely important. Without it, the evaluation would have been extremely difficult; certainly, sensitivity of measures would have been compromised.
- Natural experimental methods can be extremely powerful in detecting media campaign effects, including dose-response relationships.
- Media campaigns must account for environmental context, including related media and marketing that may reach the target audience.
- Future media evaluations would benefit from combining multiple design elements, including natural experiments under real-world conditions (as in truth®) and efficacy studies using experimental designs.
- It is important to collect data on other external interventions and policies that could confound the effects of the intervention being evaluated.

In this chapter, we noted several ways in which media evaluation in general and the truth® evaluation in particular differed from the EPIC model and other domains of evaluation. These differences can be summarized in three points. First, media evaluators are removed from the target population or audience for the media campaign. So, for example, media evaluators are not directly involved in *assessing context,* such as identifying the target audience, developing messages, and choosing media channels through which to deliver a media campaign.

Second, media evaluators directly relate to media campaign designers and developers for important evaluation steps, including gathering reconnaissance and engaging stakeholders. The relationship between evaluators and developers of media campaigns is critical to the success of media evaluations and to campaign implementation insofar as evaluation data are used for feedback and continuous improvement.

Third, because media campaign developers act as an intermediary between evaluators and campaign target audiences, process evaluation of campaign development plans and activities is crucial. Such evaluation can be formal (e.g., in-depth interviews done with truth® developers that revealed the campaign's branding strategy) or informal (e.g., participating in meetings with campaign designers to understand ads and ad messages for use in developing survey questions). For media evaluators to develop sensitive designs, methods, and measures, they need to have an in-depth understanding of how campaign developers are planning and executing strategy.

CONCLUSION

The truth® campaign evaluation was based on a natural experimental design, a form of quasi-experiment (Rossi & Freeman, 1993). Though the design did not involve any experimental manipulation of conditions, it took advantage of natural variation in media buying and hence audience exposure to truth® messages. Higher and lower GRPs in DMAs across the United States were used as natural controls to compare the effects of higher and lower campaign exposure on tobacco-related attitudes, beliefs, and behavioral outcomes.

As described in detail above, the truth® evaluation required a number of critical design decisions and compromises. Most of these were determined by the context of the evaluation in general and the campaign design, development, and launch in particular. First, the truth® campaign was launched nationally with a major media buy in DMAs across the country. The advantage of this approach for evaluators was that the campaign generated high levels of exposure and thus a large number of potential survey respondents who had seen or heard about the campaign. The disadvantage was that there was no opportunity for experimental control.

Second, campaign advertisements and messages changed over time. This required the use of multiple evaluation methodologies (e.g., process evaluation, media tracking, measurement, and addition of multiple process and outcome variables over time) and ongoing interaction and feedback between campaign designers and evaluators. The evaluation measures and instruments required continuous updating, which were generally successful due to a sound process for making modifications. However, this presented a challenge that future media evaluations should address: changing measures over time affects potential time series and requires decisions along the way in terms of which variables to keep and which to cut as the campaign develops.

Third, analyses of dose-response are critical for determining media campaign effectiveness. The truth® evaluation faced challenges in developing methods to evaluate dose-response both in the absence of experimental control and due to declining prevalence of youth smoking during the evaluation. The evaluation developed innovative methods for analyzing dose-response relationships that can serve as valuable tools for future media evaluations.

REFERENCES

Bauer, U. E., Johnson, T. M., Hopkins, R. S., & Brooks, R. G. (2000). Changes in youth cigarette use and intentions following implementation of a tobacco control program: Findings from the Florida youth tobacco survey, 1998–2000. *Journal of the American Medical Association, 284*(6), 723–728.

Borden, N. (1964). The concept of the marketing mix. *Journal of Advertising Research, 4*(6), 2–7.

Columbia Marketing Panel. (1996). *Tobacco counter-marketing strategy recommendations* (Draft report). New York: Mailman School of Public Health, Columbia University.

Evans, W. D. (2006). How social marketing works in health care. *British Medical Journal, 332*(7551), 1207–1210.

Evans, W. D., & Hastings, G. (2008). Public health branding: Recognition, promise, and delivery of healthy lifestyles. In W. D. Evans & G. Hastings (Eds.), *Public health branding: Applying marketing for social change* (pp. 475–492). London: Oxford University Press.

Evans, W. D., Price, S., & Blahut, S. (2005). Evaluating the truth brand. *Journal of Health Communication, 10*(2), 181–192.

Evans, W. D., Wasserman, J., Bertolotti, E., & Martino, S. (2002). Branding behavior: The strategy behind the truth campaign. *Social Marketing Quarterly, 8*(3), 17–29.

Farrelly, M. C., Davis, K. C., Haviland, M. L., Messeri, P., & Healton, C. G. (2005). Evidence of a dose-response relationship between "truth" antismoking ads and youth smoking prevalence. *American Journal of Public Health, 95*(3), 425–431.

Farrelly, M. C., Healton, C. G., Davis, K. C., Messeri, P., Hersey, J. C., & Haviland, M. L. (2002). Getting to the truth: Evaluating national tobacco countermarketing campaigns. *American Journal of Public Health, 92*(6), 901–907.

Freimuth, V., Cole, G., & Kirby, S. (2001). Issues in evaluating mass media health communication campaigns. In I. Rootman et al. (Eds.), *Evaluation in health promotion: Principles and perspectives* (pp. 475–492). Geneva: WHO Regional Publications, European Series, No. 92.

Goldman, L. K., & Glantz, S. A. (1998). Evaluation of antismoking advertising campaigns. *Journal of the American Medical Association, 279*(10), 772–777.

Hornik, R. C. (2002). *Public health communication: Evidence for behavior change.* Mahwah, NJ: Lawrence Erlbaum.

Kotler, P., & Andreasen, A. (1996). *Strategic marketing for nonprofit organizations.* New York: Prentice Hall.

Kotler, P., & Zaltman, G. (1971). Social marketing: An approach to planned social change. *Journal of Marketing, 35*(3), 3–12.

McKenna, J., Gutierrez, K., & McCall, K. (2000). Strategies for an effective youth counter-marketing program: Recommendations from commercial marketing experts. *Journal of Public Health Management and Practice, 6*(3), 7–13.

Petty, R. E., & Cacioppo, J. T. (1986). *Communication and persuasion: Central and peripheral routes to attitude change.* New York: Springer-Verlag.

Rossi, P. H., & Freeman, H. E. (1993). *Evaluation: A systematic approach* (5th ed.). Newbury Park, CA: Sage.

Sly, D. F., Hopkins, R. S., Trapido, E., & Ray, S. (2001). Influence of a counter-advertising media campaign on initiation of smoking: The Florida "truth" campaign. *American Journal of Public Health, 91*(2), 233–238.

Snyder, L. B., & Hamilton, M. A. (2002). Meta-analysis of U.S. health campaign effects on behavior: Emphasize enforcement, exposure, and new information, and beware the secular trend. In R. Hornik (Ed.), *Public health communication: Evidence for behavior change* (pp. 357–383). Hillsdale, NJ: Lawrence Erlbaum.

U.S. Department of Health and Human Services. (2000, November). *Healthy people 2010: Understanding and improving health* (2nd ed.). Washington, DC: U.S. Government Printing Office.

7

PROGRAM EVALUATION PLANNING

Overview and Analysis

Marc A. Zimmerman and Debra J. Holden

This book emphasizes the importance of the background work necessary to conduct effective, informative, and useful evaluations. The EPIC model we present here is intended to highlight some of the critical steps in this planning process. Although these steps are presented in linear fashion, the various steps in the planning process are more integrated and cyclical. Processes within steps may be overlapping because the information from one step is often applied in the next step, and steps later in the process are used to inform or revise products from earlier steps. The stakeholder advisory group, for example, is revisited throughout this process. The group provides vital commentary about the program and evaluation design that is necessary as the EPIC model steps are worked through. In some cases, the first step might be developing the stakeholder group and defining its roles, and assessing context and gathering reconnaissance may occur later than presented in the model. The main take-home message is that many steps prior to designing and conducting an evaluation are not usually discussed. Most evaluation reports describe the methods and results with little, if any, information about the extensive work that goes into planning. This book, however, stops at the stage in an evaluation that gets most of the attention: final evaluation design, implementation, and dissemination. We propose that if evaluators attend to the steps outlined in this book, following those that are relevant to the context, then the evaluation implementation will be much easier to initiate than without such a process. Using tools and processes described in this book will provide evaluators with prioritized evaluation questions and client input such that designing the evaluation will be fairly straightforward.

The case studies were designed to provide the reader with examples of how the EPIC model was applied to different program types and settings. Just as we expect the EPIC model to be a heuristic or conceptual toolbox to guide the evaluation process, we also intend the case studies to provide readers with an idea of the developmental process and effort that go on behind the evaluations we most often read about. No two evaluations are exactly the same, even if they are in a similar context (e.g., educational setting, service organization) or focus on the same outcomes (e.g., health status or behavior, organizational functioning). They can differ in so many ways that readers are cautioned against a formulaic approach when planning for an evaluation in any one of the settings included in the case studies. It is possible (perhaps likely), for example, that some of the issues described in one of the case studies is applicable to a different context. Many issues vary from one program to another, even if they are the same type of program, so it is virtually impossible to apply the ideas presented in the EPIC model in a linear and rigid fashion.

We identified five general steps in the evaluation planning process—assess context, gather reconnaissance, engage stakeholders, describe the program, and focus the evaluation—that provide a guideline for evaluators as they develop an evaluation plan. The EPIC model provides a heuristic for evaluation planning rather than a specified set of steps that are required for all evaluations. Some parts of the model may be more or less applicable, depending on such issues as the type of evaluation, the setting of the evaluation, the outcomes of interest, and the sponsor's interests. Thus, the EPIC model can be used as a kind of instruction guide to prepare for a program evaluation. The four case studies were chosen to represent different planning issues and provide examples of the planning process in different settings.

As expected, the EPIC model did not fit each case in the same way, and some parts of the EPIC model were more relevant than others across the cases. In this respect, evaluation planning is similar to many human endeavors. Painting a room in a house, for example, requires preparatory work that differs depending on the type and characteristics of a room. Yet the basic principles for preparing the room for the application of paint (i.e., implementation of the evaluation design in our case) need to be considered. Prepainting work may involve cleaning the walls, stripping wallpaper, filling cracks, applying primer, and caulking. But not all of these steps may be necessary for every room painted. Nevertheless, knowing about the full array of prepainting tasks that may be necessary allows the painter to decide what is required for a particular job. The care taken in this preparatory work largely will define the quality of the paint job. A brief overview of the EPIC model as applied in the case examples is provided below.

SUMMARY OF APPLICATIONS OF THE EPIC MODEL

Assess Context

One of the first tasks for evaluators in planning an evaluation is assessing the context in which the evaluation will occur, the role and relationship of the evaluator with those in the setting, and the level of analysis that the evaluation sponsors expect. This includes understanding the organizational and political environment because different contexts may require different information, procedures for obtaining the information, and ways to consider how the information will guide the planning process. The evaluator can learn about the context from a variety of sources, including Web sites, meeting minutes, annual reports, and formal or informal interviews with staff and clients. The assessment may also include sources outside the organization, such as media sources (e.g., newspaper articles) and interviews with colleagues (and competitors). The common theme across the case examples was that some initial information about the context in which the evaluation was to occur is necessary in determining the organization's commitment to the evaluation and the issues that need to be addressed to provide the most useful findings. The contextual assessment may include analysis of the organization's mission statement, funding sources, and administrative structure (Chapter 4) while for others the sources of information might include information gathering through observation or face-to-face discussions (Chapter 5). We saw that it may be vital to obtain perspectives of interested parties outside the context, such as colleagues from partner organizations or parents (Chapter 3). Yet, some contexts may not require the same depth of assessment of the organizational context because the evaluation is focused on something in the public domain, such as a media evaluation (Chapter 6).

We also found that the process of assessing the context requires attention to the evaluator and sponsor relationship, as well as the level of the evaluation. The relationship between the evaluator and the sponsor will be defined differently depending on whether the evaluator is internal or external to the program (or organization) being evaluated. The nature of the relationship may also have significant effects on the type and purpose of the evaluation. External evaluators are assumed to be more impartial than internal evaluators; because they have no stake in the evaluation results, their findings are more likely to be accepted as objective and valid. Organizations often desire impartiality because they may want to make changes and see an evaluation as being potentially helpful in guiding decision making. This is one reason why program staff may distrust the evaluation and become less than cooperative in planning and implementing it. Conversely, internal evaluators may struggle to gain credibility that their evaluation is indeed an accurate and unbiased assessment because of an inherent conflict of interest. Thus, an internal evaluator must balance being overly critical of colleagues with providing a useful assessment of the program to superiors. In Chapter 5, Reischl and Franzen describe some of the challenges involved in being an internal evaluator and some strategies used to avoid potential conflicts of interest and to maintain credibility.

The relationship of the internal or external evaluator to program staff and the evaluation sponsor also raises issues about the underlying agenda for the evaluation, how the evaluation will be used, and the access the evaluator will have to necessary data to provide a complete analysis of the program. One way to establish a productive relationship is to use a participatory approach in which evaluators and the sponsor make all important decisions together and plan the evaluation collaboratively (Chapter 4). Including more frontline staff in the planning process is another way to establish a collaborative relationship. Compared to evaluations with less stakeholder involvement, a participatory approach may help develop trust and cooperation because sponsors and staff may have more confidence that the data collected are relevant for honest assessment, and the application of the findings for decision making will have more credibility within the organization. Yet, a participatory approach may be less likely to reveal either areas of contention or important sources of information because participants may try to shape the evaluation to minimize discovery of potentially negative information. Thus, evaluators who use a participatory approach need to guard against getting biased impressions and misinformation. Reischl and Franzen (Chapter 5) provide a good example of the balance that may be necessary in being participatory but also defining parameters of the evaluation process and design.

External evaluators may also have their own ideas about what needs to be done and how to do it and may initiate the planning process by addressing questions they perceive as the most important, without engaging stakeholders to the extent expected by the sponsor. This scenario may translate into more effort for the evaluator to build relationships with the stakeholders in order to assure them that their input will be incorporated into the planning process. Some balance between complete independence and initial relationship building and some participatory processes with all stakeholders during the planning phase of an evaluation often helps provide the balance necessary to implement the most useful and effective evaluations.

The process of establishing relationships between evaluators and the sponsor and program staff will help define the level of the evaluation. Establishing the level early in the evaluation process is important because it defines the type of information to be collected and directs conversations about how the data will be obtained. It also indicates the evaluation's goals. In most cases, the evaluation will require information across levels, including individual clients, program staff, and organizational structures and functions. Whatever the level of a particular evaluation, it is necessary to identify and understand this aspect of the intervention during the planning process. If not, the evaluator will have to fill in information gaps as the evaluation is taking place, and this may delay completion of the evaluation, take attention and time away from other aspects of evaluation implementation (e.g., data collection, analysis), and require evaluators to work in a more haphazard fashion. Therefore, it is important for the evaluator to remain flexible and be prepared to solve problems quickly as they arise.

Gather Reconnaissance

The next step in the EPIC model is to investigate and understand the motivations behind the request for an evaluation. Exploring the intended uses of the evaluation is one way to understand the motivations for the evaluation. The evaluator needs to be an astute listener and incisive questioner to get past the rhetoric and jargon that often permeate explanations for evaluations. An evaluation is inevitably threatening to someone or some program even if that is not the sponsor's intention. Therefore, it is vital to learn about the evaluation's underlying purpose. Many issues often come to light once the intended uses of the evaluation are stated explicitly. Yet it is vital that evaluators not form conclusions too quickly and to ensure that their perceptions are accurate. This requires explicit efforts to gain multiple perspectives and confirm that the impressions are based in fact and verifiable (i.e., valid). It also means that evaluators may need to make their own expectations known and help stakeholders understand how the evaluation findings can be used to inform program development. Knowing about the issues and the intended application of the evaluation ahead of time is beneficial because it may help inform additional data that may need to be collected, plan for additional sources of data for different information, and anticipate problems with reporting the results.

Validating stakeholders' perspectives not only helps tailor the evaluation to address the unique circumstances of the program but also increases the chances for greater cooperation and more useful data. In some cases, the evaluation is required by the funding agency, so validating perspectives among stakeholders may be less relevant than for evaluations that are designed to improve a program or are otherwise not required. Regardless of the evaluation setting, it is critical for the evaluator to listen to stakeholders, educate stakeholders about the usefulness of the findings, and develop strategies that address their concerns. Perhaps the most effective way to validate perspectives is to use a participatory approach to engender support and buy-in by stakeholders and the program staff. Thus, the evaluator may need to develop strategies for involving interested parties to determine shared ideas on applying evaluation findings for program planning and to help resolve conflicting expectations regarding their use (i.e., ensure that everyone is on the same page).

Engage Stakeholders

The process of engaging stakeholders begins with defining partners and their roles and developing procedures for working together. Stakeholders can help ensure the study is relevant and valid for the context, gain cooperation among staff to conduct the evaluation, and apply the findings for program development. In addition, engaging stakeholders is a matter of social justice. The stakeholders have more of a vested interest in the outcomes of the evaluation than the evaluator, so involving them in the process is respectful and ethical. A key issue in this process, however, is identifying who the key stakeholders are, and motivating them to participate in the evaluation planning. Deciding which stakeholders to invite depends on many factors, including the setting and level of the program being evaluated, the skills and experience of the evaluator, the relationship between the sponsor and the evaluator, and the larger community context. The case examples provide a range of approaches for identifying and engaging them. The stakeholders might include the sponsor, the staff, the recipients of the program, and others external to the program being evaluated. Engaging the stakeholders is most often dependent on the relationship evaluators establish with those involved with the evaluation, making the planning process all the more important for developing relevant, accepted, and useful evaluations.

It is noteworthy that evaluations of programs for children (in or out of school settings) may need to involve parents. Parents' interest in their children can be passionate, and involving them in the planning process may be vital for the success of the evaluation. In an educational context, however, applying the evaluation results may be especially constrained by the social and political dynamics in which the program is embedded. Thus, engaging a broadly representative group of stakeholders (e.g., parents, teachers, administrators, school board members) when working in a public education context may be especially important. Student voices may also be especially helpful.

Stakeholders play a somewhat different role when they are essentially the funding agency because they may view themselves as having a conflict of interest. They also may feel entitled to define the parameters of the evaluation because they are funding both the program being evaluated and the evaluation. In these cases, it is especially crucial for the evaluator to clearly define roles and make it clear that the evaluation must be independent and objective. Thus, in these situations engaging stakeholders may actually require restraining their involvement to some degree while also advocating for involvement of others outside of the funding agency, including staff, consumers, and community leaders. This is one reason why establishing an honest and open relationship with sponsors and clearly communicating one's expectations are so important in the early phases of evaluation planning.

Once the key stakeholders are identified and invited, evaluators need a process for engagement that includes procedures for decision making, strategies for communicating, and establishment of meeting schedules and rules of conduct. The case examples provide a wide range of strategies that may be partly a result of the specific setting and partly a function of the sponsoring agency, but all of the authors address the need to define the roles of the stakeholders as they become engaged in the planning process. Defining the roles can be done by using a brief procedures checklist or manual that specifies such items as the frequency of meetings, the procedures for agenda setting, leadership for organizing and running the meeting, along with specific goals of the group. Flexibility is a useful trait while conducting an evaluation, but it may be especially important during the planning phase because this is when conflicts among engaged stakeholders with regard to their own agenda and values will be most evident. The evaluator has to be a diplomat and be prepared to be both responsive to issues raised and steadfast in methodological rigor.

Describe the Program

As we learned from the case examples, it was vital for each evaluation to gain a deep understanding of the program being evaluated. This may involve learning about the program's history and how it was established, its stage of development, and how it changed over time. Evaluators can learn about the program from a variety of sources, including archival data in the organization (e.g., meeting minutes, grant proposals, business plans, logic models), informal interviews with current and former staff and administrators, and external informants and sources, such as community leaders, newspaper accounts, and consumers. In the process of collecting information about the program, evaluators may need to fill in gaps with their own impressions and then validate what was learned with stakeholders. This is an important step in the planning process because it can provide information about areas that require more attention than others, help identify hidden agendas, and inform the design necessary to provide an accurate and useful assessment of the program. It may be especially useful to develop a logic model for the program that key stakeholders agree on to understand how the program was intended to operate and to provide direction for the evaluation itself. This can provide a useful starting point to begin discussions about what factors to focus on in the evaluation, what measures to use, and what sources of information are best suited for the outcomes being assessed.

A central issue regarding program evaluation is the stage of development of the program. Newer programs may require a different approach than programs that have been operating for some time. Newer programs may request an evaluation to help them manage the program more efficiently, mobilize resources for expansion, or determine what direction to take once the program is actually up and running. In these instances, an evaluation may be viewed as an organizational development tool. For older programs, the results of the evaluation may actually define the shape of its future (e.g., resources received), including its very survival. As we learned from the case examples, these are often more delicate situations that the evaluator needs to learn about in the planning process.

Focus the Evaluation

At the final stage of the planning process, evaluators test out their ideas for the evaluation design. Feasibility and consent from stakeholders is necessary before implementation. This is the time to put into writing the actual plan and operationalize questions to be asked and measures to be used. This is also the stage of the planning process when the evaluator shares an evaluation plan to clearly specify and link resources needed to carry out the evaluation, the evaluation activities, and its short- and long-term outcomes. The case examples provide useful lessons for how to build consensus with stakeholders and for gaining their endorsement for the evaluation design. The feasibility of the design is typically a central focus of these discussions. This includes practical issues such as minimizing burden on staff to complete data collection tasks and recruiting consumers to obtain information from them, and analysis of the types of questions being asked and whether they will garner the information intended in ways that are consistent with organizational and local culture, norms, and values. In this stage, evaluators need to be clear about what the evaluation can and cannot achieve. Evaluators might discuss the evaluation logic model and explain the choices made for the design by linking different aspects of the methods to specific findings that were discovered during the earlier phases of the planning process.

LESSONS LEARNED

Our hope is that the EPIC model provides evaluators with the conceptual tools and a framework for thinking about the pre-evaluation tasks that may be necessary for a successful, useful, and informative evaluation. Done thoughtfully, efforts in the planning stage will help avoid pitfalls later during implementation and reporting. Attention to the planning process for an evaluation helps ensure an evaluation enjoys the cooperation of the stakeholders involved in the evaluation, generates valid data that are appropriate to answering the questions that initiated the evaluation in the first place, and provides useful information that serves its intended purpose. Thoughtful evaluation planning may also help evaluators gain a better understanding of the context in which an evaluation is being conducted, allowing for the selection of relevant measures that would be most valuable in applying evaluation results for future program planning and resource allocation. Notably, when the planning process involves the interested parties (e.g., stakeholders, staff, participants), the results are more likely to be considered in an open-minded and honest discussion that is most useful for program improvement and decision making. Effective and organized efforts in the planning process can help to avoid conflict with stakeholders and sponsors once the evaluation is complete.

We hope that the field will begin to pay more attention to issues that will influence the success of an evaluation. For the most part, the issues to consider during the evaluation planning process inevitably will come up some time during an evaluation project. Whether it is done during the planning phases of an evaluation, addressed during implementation of the design, or confronted once the evaluation is completed and the results are presented, the issues of context, cooperation, validity, and usefulness undoubtedly will come up. When the planning issues are confronted during implementation, they can distract from efficient data collection, stall the schedule of activities, or completely derail efforts to gain valuable information because evaluators will have to back-track and explain the purpose of the evaluation, clarify why specific questions are asked, spend time encouraging participation, and develop strategies to ensure that the data obtained are valid and useful. If the planning issues come up during the reporting of results, it may be too late to save the application of the results for program development because the validity of the data will be questioned, the applicability of the design to answer the questions that drove the decision to do an evaluation will be suspect, and the integrity of the evaluation will be compromised. Like most human endeavors, attention to details during the planning phases of the activity will help increase the probability of success, help avoid surprises, and provide a basis (a constituency) for addressing unplanned events.

CONCLUSION

Our goal for this book is to give attention to an often ignored or minimally attended to aspect of program evaluation that often defines its success. Most textbooks and training in evaluation focus on design issues and application of the results (Bamberger, Rugh, & Mabry 2006; Berk & Rossi, 1998; Patton, 1997; Rossi, Lipsey, & Freeman, 2004; Wholey, Hatry, & Newcomer, 1994). While this is unarguably necessary, important, and central to the field of program evaluation, it neglects the vital initial phases of the evaluation process. The case examples in this book demonstrate the utility and importance of evaluation planning regardless of the context or topic of the evaluation. They also illustrate that even though evaluation planning may differ across settings, it provides the foundation upon which all evaluations are based. Whether or not an evaluator intentionally and systematically engages in the planning process, the issues that are part of the planning process will have significant effects on the tenor of the relationship between evaluator and sponsor and the applicability of the evaluation.

We end the book with EPIC rules of order for evaluation planning. We hope that these ideas will help guide you in your preparatory work for evaluations you conduct in the future.

- Rule 1: Understand the program and be sure the stakeholders understand you.
- Rule 2: Know what the outcomes of interest are.
- Rule 3: Identify a broad-based group of stakeholders to guide the evaluation.

- Rule 4: Define roles and expectations early in the process.
- Rule 5: Create procedures to obtain stakeholder feedback and support.
- Rule 6: Learn about the history and evolution of the program to be evaluated.
- Rule 7: Obtain multiple perspectives about the program.
- Rule 8: Assess the organization context, norms, and values before evaluating it.
- Rule 9: Consider the use and dissemination of the results from the beginning.
- Rule 10: Don't follow too many rules; be flexible in your thinking and thoughtful in your planning.

REFERENCES

Bamberger, M., Rugh, J., & Mabry, L. (2006). *Real world evaluation.* Thousand Oaks, CA: Sage.

Berk, R., & Rossi, P. (1998). *Thinking about program evaluation.* Thousand Oaks, CA: Sage.

Patton, M. Q. (1997). *Utilization-focused evaluation: The new century text* (3rd ed.). Thousand Oaks, CA: Sage.

Rossi, P. H., Lipsey, M. W., & Freeman, H. E. (2004). *Evaluation: A systematic approach* (7th ed.). Thousand Oaks, CA: Sage.

Wholey, J. S., Hatry, H. P., & Newcomer, K. E. (Eds.). (1994). *Handbook of practical program evaluation.* San Francisco: Jossey-Bass.

INDEX

ABOUT THE EDITORS

Debra J. Holden, PhD, is director of RTI International's Community Health Promotion Research Program. She has nearly 19 years of experience conducting evaluations of public health programs at the local, state, and national level, including evaluations of programs for agencies such as the Centers for Disease Control and Prevention (CDC) and the Centers for Medicare & Medicaid Services (CMS). As a community health psychologist, she has led numerous program evaluations and has become known among CDC and other federal agencies for her evaluation planning tools and techniques. She is currently leading evaluation planning for the National Cancer Institute's Community Cancer Centers Program (NCCCP), a pilot program being implemented in 16 community hospitals. She also is leading evaluation planning for CDC's Comprehensive Cancer Control Program, a national program being implemented through states, territories, and tribes in the United States. She recently completed an evaluation plan for CDC's Colorectal Cancer Screening Demonstration Program and an evaluation for the start-up period of the program, with findings published in two manuscripts in *Preventing Chronic Disease* (March 2008). She has worked with the American Cancer Society, American Social Health Association, and the North Carolina Department of Health and Human Services (as well as six other state health departments) to plan for an evaluation of one or more programs. Drs. Holden and Zimmerman collaborated on a 2004 special issue of *Health Education & Behavior,* titled "Application of Youth Empowerment Theory to Tobacco Control," which Dr. Holden coedited with Dr. Peter Messeri from Columbia University. She recently completed a chapter of a book, as an invited author, that focuses on the youth empowerment lessons learned. The book, *Lighting a Fuse for Public Health: Tobacco Control Lessons Learned,* will be published by JSI Publishers in 2009.

Marc A. Zimmerman, PhD, is professor and chair in the Department of Health Behavior and Health Education at the University of Michigan, School of Public Health. He is also a professor in the Department of Psychology and the Combined Program in Education and Psychology at the University of Michigan and a research scientist in the Center for Human Growth and Development. Dr. Zimmerman is the director of the Centers for Disease Control (CDC)–funded Prevention Research Center of Michigan, which includes several evaluation studies. He is principal investigator on a CDC-funded youth violence prevention program, Youth Empowerment Solutions, designed to involve youth in community change activities, and on a National Institute on Drug Abuse–funded Flint Adolescent Study, a 12-year longitudinal study of ninth graders. He is editor of *Health Education & Behavior* and a member of the editorial board for *Health Education Research.* Dr. Zimmerman's primary research has focused on empowerment theory and the study of adolescent health and resiliency. His research has consistently focused on individual and community assets, resiliency, and community-based research methods. He has published more than 100 peer-reviewed and invited papers and book chapters on a wide variety of topics, including adolescent mental health, school outcomes, social relationships, racial identity, youth violence, sexual behavior, and substance abuse; HIV/AIDS prevention; and empowerment theory. In 1995, he coedited *AIDS Prevention in the Community: Lessons from the First Decade,* published by the American Public Health Association, which reported on the evaluation of the Robert Wood Johnson Foundation AIDS prevention initiative. Dr. Zimmerman has been involved in program implementation and evaluation for more than 20 years. He received his PhD in psychology from the University of Illinois and a master's degree in interdisciplinary studies from the University of Oregon.

ABOUT THE CONTRIBUTORS

Kevin C. Davis, MA, is an economist in RTI International's Public Health Policy Research Program. His research focuses on the evaluation of public health social marketing campaigns. Mr. Davis has contributed to many studies examining the effects of tobacco countermarketing campaigns on smoking-related outcomes among youth, HIV prevention campaigns and messaging, social marketing campaigns aimed at promoting parent-child communication, and campaigns aimed at curbing obesity. Mr. Davis's research has also focused on the development and use of measures to assess audience reaction and receptivity to health marketing advertisements. He has published in peer-reviewed journals, including the *Journal of Adolescent Health, Journal of Communication, Nicotine & Tobacco Research, American Journal of Public Health,* and *Tobacco Control.* He has also authored or coauthored technical reports for the New York State Department of Health, the American Legacy Foundation, and the Centers for Disease Control and Prevention. He received bachelor's degrees in history and economics from the University of North Carolina at Asheville and a master's degree in applied economics from the University of North Carolina at Greensboro.

W. Douglas Evans, PhD, is professor and Director of Health Communication and Marketing in the School of Public Health and Health Services at George Washington University. Dr. Evans has 16 years of experience in prevention research, health promotion and disease prevention program evaluation, and social marketing and communications research. He specializes in the design and evaluation of health behavior change and public education intervention programs to communicate science-based information to diverse audiences. He has published more than 50 peer-reviewed articles and chapters on health risk behavior, including the effects of social marketing on behavior change and translation of commercial marketing strategies into public health. He edited *Public Health Branding: Applying Marketing for Social Change* (2008), published by Oxford University Press. Dr. Evans has worked extensively on public health subject areas of tobacco control; nutrition, physical activity, and obesity; diabetes; HIV/STDs; and reproductive health. His most recent evaluation research focuses on obesity prevention social marketing using an ecological framework. This work includes randomized controlled studies of prevention interventions in Chicago and in the Western Cape region of South Africa. Dr. Evans received a PhD and an MA in cognitive science from the Johns Hopkins University and a bachelor's degree in psychology/philosophy from Reed College.

Matthew C. Farrelly, PhD, is director of RTI International's Public Health Policy Research Program. His primary research focus is on evaluating state and national tobacco control programs, including antismoking campaigns, smoke-free laws, cigarette excise taxes, and community-based interventions. His research has demonstrated that the national truth® antismoking campaign was successful in changing youth's tobacco-related attitudes, intentions, and behavior. He also has found that higher cigarette prices and investments in state tobacco control programs are associated with decreased youth and adult smoking as well as cigarette sales. In addition, Dr. Farrelly has investigated whether attempts to curb the use of one substance, such as tobacco, have the unintended consequence of encouraging marijuana or alcohol use. Dr. Farrelly has published extensively in peer-reviewed journals, including the *American Economic Review, American Journal of Public Health, Economic Inquiry, Health Economics, Health Education & Behavior, Journal of Health Economics, Journal of the National Cancer Institute, Nicotine & Tobacco Research, Preventive Medicine, RAND Journal of Economics, Southern Economic Journal,* and *Tobacco Control.* He received his PhD in economics from the University of Maryland.

Susan P. Franzen, MS, is an evaluation associate in the Prevention Research Center at the University of Michigan, School of Public Health. She has conducted community-based evaluations for coalitions, foundations, and university projects. Ms. Franzen's research has focused on evaluating programs designed to reduce racial disparities in infant mortality, promote "friendly" patient-provider relationships, empower youth to work with neighborhood adults to create and sustain community improvement projects, and implement a systems-based community change model. She is currently evaluating beautification grants for a local foundation. Ms. Franzen earned a bachelor's degree and a master's degree in health education from the University of Michigan–Flint.

Julie A. Marshall, PhD, is director of the Centers for Disease Control and Prevention (CDC)–funded Rocky Mountain Prevention Research Center and Professor of Epidemiology and Community Health at the University of Colorado–Denver, School of Medicine. Dr. Marshall has been a coinvestigator on the San Luis Valley Health Studies in southern Colorado since their inception in 1981. She has published articles on diet and risk of obesity, insulin resistance and Type 2 diabetes, indicators of nutritional risk in the elderly, how genetic variation modifies the relation between diet and blood cholesterol, and analytic methods. She teaches advanced epidemiological methods to PhD and MSPH students, serves on thesis and dissertation committees, and is mentor on three young investigator career awards. Her recent work has focused on translating research into practice by working with community members to identify the important research questions and develop and implement intervention and evaluation methods for prevention of obesity and Type 2 diabetes. She is currently funded by CDC, the National Institutes of Health, and the Robert Wood Johnson Foundation for studies in school and family settings. Dr. Marshall is interested in understanding environmental and social factors that influence people's daily choices regarding diet and physical activity and how the public health system can be designed to better support local-level, data-driven decision making and community-level resolution of health indicators. She received a master's degree in public health from the University of Hawaii as an East-West Center Scholar and a PhD in epidemiology from the University of Washington.

Mari Millery, PhD, is an associate research scientist at Columbia University's Mailman School of Public Health. Dr. Millery has worked with a variety of public health service programs, both as an internal and external evaluator. Her areas of expertise include HIV/AIDS, substance abuse, adolescent health, and continuing education of health providers. Many of her projects focus on issues of health information use and information technologies. As the internal evaluation director of two large multisite HIV/AIDS service programs, she facilitates the planning of focused evaluation studies in close collaboration with program staff. She also works with other service programs, including a cancer patient information service and a technology-based hypertension program, leading the evaluation planning process as an external evaluation partner. She received her PhD in psychology from the City University of New York.

Thomas M. Reischl, PhD, is an associate research scientist at the University of Michigan, School of Public Health. He serves as the evaluation director of the Prevention Research Center of Michigan. His research interests focus on the development and evaluation of community-based public health programs, family support programs, and consumer-controlled (self-/mutual-help) programs. Recent and current projects include evaluation studies of neighborhood-based violence prevention projects, community-based infant mortality prevention projects, youth employment programs, an intervention for nonresident fathers and their sons, public health preparedness training programs, and a mutual-help organization for persons with schizophrenia. He earned a bachelor's degree in psychology from St. Olaf College and a master's degree and a PhD in community psychology from the University of Illinois at Urbana–Champaign.